EARLY PROTESTANT EDUCATORS

The Educational Writings of Martin Luther,
John Calvin, and Other Leaders of
Protestant Thought

By

FREDERICK EBY, Ph.D., Ll.D.

*Professor of the History and Philosophy of Education
The University of Texas*

AMS PRESS
NEW YORK

Reprinted from the edition of 1931, New York
First AMS EDITION published 1971
Manufactured in the United States of America

International Standard Book Number: 0-404-02238

Library of Congress Number: 76-149656

AMS PRESS INC.
NEW YORK, N. Y. 10003

PREFACE

THE tendency to utilize source materials in the teaching of any form of historical truth in college classes is increasingly apparent. It must be regarded as a happy omen, for it is unquestionably in accordance with the soundest principles of educational method. The history of education has never been entirely lacking in the use of such original sources. From the Renaissance onward attention was constantly directed to the educational writings of Plato, Aristotle, Plutarch, Cicero, Quintilian, and others. In more recent days the Germans have been most active in rendering the later sources accessible. Not so much has been done in America, though Henry Barnard published materials of the greatest value, and some others have edited individual works of great service to the study of the history of education.

The editing of a source book is not without its problems. One of the chief of these problems is the adapting of the work to the greatest use of the general student who has not the time to search through masses of material for a few facts pertinent to the inquiry he has before him. Again, there must be something to capture and sustain attention. Because the materials are sources does not necessarily endow them with vivid interest for the general reader. Of course it is entirely different with the specialist. He has the eyes to see and the background of knowledge to interpret and understand. As to just what materials to include, the particular form of presentation, what forewords, notes, references, and other interpretative suggestions should be included are all questions pressing for decision. Whether these issues should be decided from the standpoint of the specialist, or of the novice making his first survey of the history of education, is highly important. As a strictly scientific procedure it is better to present each piece of source material as it came from the brain and hands of the author and permit the reader to reach his own conclusion as to its historical significance. For the novice it is probably more helpful to give direction to his search, just as it is advisable to suggest to the student looking through a microscope at a biological specimen what he should expect to see. A median course has been chosen in presenting these materials, and some suggestions are made as to what these materials offer, but in every case brevity has been the governing rule.

The sketches of the lives and works of the various authors are extremely brief. It is assumed that students will have access to detailed works on the biographies of these men. It was considered wiser to use all possible space for the sources themselves.

I am very grateful for the permission to use translations of Luther's writings already in print. First my acknowlegments are made to the Concordia Publishing House of St. Louis for the privilege of reprinting two lengthy extracts

PREFACE

from Dr. F. V. N. Painter's "Luther on Education." Secondly, The United Lutheran Publishing House of Philadelphia has generously consented to permit the republication of a number of letters from Luther's "Correspondence and Other Contemporary Letters" by Preserved Smith, Ph.D., and Charles M. Jacobs, D.D.

I make most cordial acknowledgment of valuable assistance rendered by several friends. Dr. Albert Henry Newman, the celebrated church historian, has kindly given expert help in locating certain passages and also in the translation of parts of several of the school orders. My thanks are due also to Mr. E. W. Winkler, librarian of the University of Texas, for assistance in securing books, and to Miss Lena Strackbein for typing the manuscript.

FREDERICK EBY.

THE UNIVERSITY OF TEXAS,
AUSTIN, TEX.
December, 1930.

CONTENTS

CONTENTS

CONTENTS

INTRODUCTION

THE sixteenth century was one of the critical epochs in human history. Beginning with the impetus imparted by the Renaissance some years earlier, a profound and far-reaching revolution occurred in northern Europe, involving the political, economic, social, and cultural as well as the ecclesiastical and religious conditions of the age. Above all else, as later became apparent, it signified the emergence into independent life and action of the Teutonic races and prepared the way for their ultimate leadership of civilization. As far as the schools and education are concerned, the revolution involved new beginnings whose importance for later centuries cannot readily be exaggerated.

The first third of the century was a period of the wildest confusion educationally and religiously, and chaos was narrowly averted by strenuous action at the critical moment. Up to the middle of the previous century scholasticism and medievalism had exercised undisputed control of the schools, both high and low. About that time the introduction of humanism inflicted deep wounds, but the inertia of the past was too great for scholastic supremacy to be easily destroyed. The enemies of the scholastic method and of the medieval mind were, however, rapidly increasing in number and power. These enemies formed three groups: the humanists, the church reformers, and the philosophical-scientific thinkers.

The humanists were radically opposed to medieval institutions and scholastic ideals of life and methods of thought. They replaced monkish Latin with the pure Latin of the ancient Roman world in their speech and writings; they abandoned the literature of the church in a wild enthusiasm for classical pagan authors. The scholastic methods of reasoning and disputation were thrown out in favor of the artistic appreciation of beauty of form and expression. But there was present a still deeper antagonism of spirit: Medievalism involved conformity to tradition and obedience to authority and the conventions of institutional life; humanism was the freest expression of individuality, of personal judgment, and action. Even though it partook greatly of the pagan spirit, humanism enjoyed the powerful support and protection of the church and was, therefore, unhampered in its assault upon the past.

The second enemy of medieval life and scholasticism was the group of religious reformers. These hurled attacks against the theological system which the scholastic philosophy had so patiently constructed and on which the church had founded its claims to infallible authority. Over against the dogma of the infallibility of the church of Rome, Luther and Calvin posited an infallible revelation given to man in the Holy Scriptures. Medieval life and morals were guided by the rules and regulations of monastery and custom; the Protestants sought guidance for all practical problems in the Bible. The same was true of all the questions of theology, philosophy, and science, for the Scriptures were the source of all truth.

A third and irresistible power was slowly rising at this time which more than anything else was to raise an insurmountable wall separating the modern from medieval modes of thought. This was the advancing scientific knowledge of the day, especially the Copernican system. Coming just at the moment when the first great inundating tide of the Protestant revolt had reached its crest, the implications of the new and startling astronomy seemed as outrageous to the Protestant leaders as they were to the followers of the traditional philosophy. But in the end Protestant theology was able to shift its philosophic basis and the medieval was not. Heliocentricity was a dagger thrust into the heart of the medieval *Weltanschauung*.

The sources gathered together here are from the great Protestant Church reformers, Luther, Bugenhagen, and Melanchthon in Germany, Calvin in Geneva, and Knox in Scotland. Zwingli, the Swiss reformer, has not been included, for his work and influence can hardly be considered a force contributing to the evolution of education which affected America. It was quite otherwise with the Anabaptists, from whose writings several excerpts have been taken. As yet these people have never been mentioned as a factor in the history of education. Their inclusion here comes more especially in connection with the presentation of the various attitudes in regard to the relation of state, church, and school. At this point their influence was important beyond question. A more exact study of their attitude toward culture may reveal other lines of influence.

The sources selected have to do especially with the founding of the elementary schools, though the Latin gymnasium is also included, and some few passages mention the universities.

In interpreting the reconstruction of education at this period it is necessary to bear in mind the schools and educational practices which were in vogue during the later middle ages. The more closely one observes the various suggestions made by the religious reformers for reconstruction the more clearly it is seen that little is absolutely original. There is, however, a shifting of emphasis and a reorganizing with a new and larger purpose in view. The institutionalism of medieval life was replaced by family discipline, by Protestant confessionalism, and by subjection to the state.

The origin of the popular elementary school well exemplifies the evolution of education at this time. German reading and writing schools had been common in the towns and cities for several centuries, especially in northern Germany and in Holland. They had come into existence in response to the increasing need of the commercial class for these arts in the conduct of business affairs. It was less and less possible to get on by employing the clergy to write letters, record contracts, and keep accounts. The local clergy opposed these schools with deep-seated animosity. They were finally tolerated only after promising to confine instruction to reading and writing and these in the vernacular tongue. Such limitations were designed to discriminate against them. They were not really schools which imparted learning and culture and prepared for advancement in life but merely training courses in these specific arts.

Some of these schools were under the control of the city councils; most of them, however, were unauthorized, taught by indigent itinerant students responsible to no one. The school codes or regulations during the Reformation require the suppression of instruction by these volunteer reading and writing masters. The reading and writing schools fostered by the cities and towns became the forerunners of the modern elementary school.

Ever since its conflict with the public schools of the pagan world in early Christian centuries, the Church tolerated no agency to control education but herself. Bitter conflict had broken out between the cities and the church authorities of northern Germany over the establishment of the burgh Latin schools and the reading and writing schools. Compromises were usually effected, but the chancellors of the cathedrals, who had always been in control of the schools of the church, continued to assert their supervisory authority. With the dawn of the Lutheran Reformation these schools suddenly declined or entirely ceased. Lutheranism swept away all the ecclesiastical officials, leaving Germany without any authorities to establish, support, and control churches and schools. To meet this threatening situation Luther turned to the secular authorities that had undertaken for several centuries to promote popular schools, the mayors and councilmen of Germany. They could now under the Protestant revolution assume full power over education, seeing that they were no longer hampered by the Catholic

Church authorities. The same obligation was placed upon the German princes to establish schools and universities throughout their principalities.

The reading and writing schools were ultimately transformed into the German folk schools. This was accomplished when the German state authorities took charge of education and promoted the establishment of elementary schools throughout the towns and villages similar to those established by the independent cities and towns. We must not fail to observe another factor in their transformation, namely, their new function and enlarged curriculum. Hitherto they had existed merely to impart a skill in reading and writing; now they were to be used as an instrument to mould German life to civic and Christian virtues. Historic culture was their new aim. This was accomplished by making the catechism, Christian doctrine, morals, and church music the central subjects. All of these changes were contained in the suggestions of the reformers.

The Latin school also underwent a change in spirit, and to a large degree in curriculum. It did not depart radically from the character which the humanistic revival had given it. It did, nevertheless, assume a Protestant attitude in its religious instruction and aimed less at Ciceronian eloquence and more at preparation for reading the Scriptures and the Church Fathers.

Both Luther and Calvin borrowed their fundamental ideals of church and state from the same source, the Old Testament, and their views were accordingly somewhat similar. But they could not work out their plans in the

6

same way. The conditions which surrounded the two reformers were very different. Luther had to deal with a large number of separate states, princes, and free cities; Calvin with a single city state. In dealing with a coherent community Calvin was enabled to realize his ideal far more easily. Luther was compelled to place the church and the school under the authority and protection of the state. Calvin on the other hand identified church and state in a single organism, a Christian theocracy. Knox and the Puritans followed Calvin's views as to the relation of state, church, and school. The Anabaptists held a wholly diverse conception, the absolute separation of church and state. This attitude brought them into direct conflict with the secular power wherever they lived and was everywhere the cause of horrible persecution. For this reason they were looked upon by Lutherans and Calvinists as not merely intolerable heretics, but as anarchists as well. Having no state to establish and maintain schools and higher institutions in which their doctrines might be taught, they were thrown back upon their own unaided efforts. The consequence was that only elementary culture had encouragement among them.

MARTIN LUTHER

LIFE AND WORK

AMONG the religious and educational thinkers and writers of the first third of the sixteenth century, Erasmus, Luther, Bugenhagen, and Melanchthon occupy the front rank. Calvin, Knox, and Loyola come a full generation later as far as their educational activities are concerned. The problem of greatest moment at that time was the reorganization of the schools in accordance with the views of those religious reformers who had put an end to the universal sway of the Roman Catholic Church, together with medieval learning, and had established a number of new confessions in the various countries of northern Europe. Among the reformers, Luther was the most aggressive religious reformer and the most extensive writer on education. Only a few facts in regard to his colorful and tempestuous career, especially as these will help to interpret his educational ideas, can be presented here.

Luther was born of humble stock, his father being a coal miner. Of his low origin he was not ashamed but rather gloried in it, and he never lost a profound sympathy for the common people and for what he conceived as their highest welfare. It was this interest which made him eager to provide for their training, especially in religion. He was born at Eisleben in 1483 and brought up at Mansfeld in Saxony where he attended his first elementary school. At fourteen he was sent to a higher school at Magdeburg and later to another at Eisenach. Being quite poor he had to sing and beg in the streets for a living. At eighteen he attended the University of Erfurt and four years later, in opposition to his father's plan for him, he became a monk in the Augustinian monastery of that place. In these institutions he acquired a vivid knowledge of the methods of instruction employed and the materials of the curriculum. The methods were extremely bad, and discipline even worse. Luther complained of being beaten inhumanly, once fifteen times in a single forenoon. In 1502 the University of Wittenberg was established by the emperor, the first German university to be founded by secular power alone. In 1508 Luther was made a professor in this institution with the duty of lecturing on the "Dialectic" and "Physics" of Aristotle. While thus engaged he studied theology and taking his degree in that subject was authorized to lecture on the Scriptures.

In 1511 Luther made a visit to Rome, and his observations of the life and conduct of the papal authorities profoundly altered his confidence in their sincerity and piety. In 1517 he nailed the celebrated ninety-five theses against indulgences to the door of the Castle church; this act is often regarded as the real initiation of the Lutheran Reformation. Three years later he issued his appeal to the German nobility to undertake a thorough reform of the entire ecclesiastical order. This scathing attack upon the numerous evils which infested the Roman Church was followed at once by a vigorous tract on "Christian Liberty" and another on "The Babylonish Captivity of the Church." From this time it was clear that his breach with the Roman curia was irreconcilable. He was brought to trial at the Diet of Worms and condemned as a heretic but was privately shielded from the punishment usually meted out to the enemies of the Roman Church. In spite of this condemnation his doctrines triumphed almost everywhere in Germany and Scandinavia. Luther died in 1546, the idol of the German people.

Luther's influence upon education has always been a subject of bitter controversy. One dispute centers about his attitude toward the higher studies and humanistic culture; another finds its focus in his relation to the rise of state popular schools.

As to the first, Erasmus declared: "Wherever Lutheranism prevails, learning and liberal culture go to the ground." In more recent times Janssen elaborates the same charge. He quotes Luther: "The universities were only worthy of being reduced to dust; nothing more hellish or devilish had ever appeared on earth from the beginning of things or ever would appear" and explains the great decline of the universities and schools as due to attacks of Luther and his followers.[1] Among the many who adopt a critical estimate

[1] JANSSEN, J., "History of the German People," Vol. I, *passim;* Vol. III, pp. 332–370; Vol. XIII, *passim.*

and who class Luther as more or less of an obscurantist are von Döllinger,[1] Paulsen,[2] Beard.[3] For a time the leaders of the humanistic movement such as Erasmus, Hutten, and Eoban Hess allied themselves with Luther in his efforts at reform. But the inner divergence of their views was irreconcilable, and in consequence the humanists fell out with him in the end.

On the opposite side, favorable estimates of Luther's attitude toward scientific and liberal culture have been equally positive. Among his admirers may be cited Faulkner,[4] Harnack,[5] and Lindsay.[6]

Equally conflicting have been the views of educators and historians in regard to Luther's services to popular education. Dr. Painter says: "Luther deserves henceforth to be recognized as the greatest, not only of religious, but of educational reformers."[7] Again, speaking of the "Letter to the Mayors" of 1524, he declares, "The address must be regarded the most important educational treatise ever writ-

[1] VON DÖLLINGER, JOHN IGNATIUS, "Die Reformation," Vol. I, p. 442.

[2] PAULSEN, F., "Geschichte des gelehrten Unterrichts," 1919 ed., Vol. I, pp. 182–184.

[3] BEARD, CHARLES, "Martin Luther and the Reformation," pp. 197–198.

[4] FAULKNER, JOHN ALFRED, "Luther and Culture," *Papers of the American Society of Church History,* Vol. VIII, pp. 149–168.

[5] HARNACK, A., "Martin Luther in seiner Bedeutung für die Geschichte der Wissenschaft und der Bildung," in *Reden und Aufsätze,* pp. 160–164, 1904.

[6] LINDSAY, T. M., "Luther and the German Reformation," pp. 234–240.

[7] PAINTER, F. V. N., "Luther on Education," p. 168.

ten,"[1] Among recent writers, Bruce concludes: "Luther, therefore, stands as the greatest educator of his age, and in the very front rank of the world's greatest educators."[2] Compayré, the distinguished French educator, is of the same opinion. German historians generally attribute almost all that is best to the efforts of Luther. Lindsay, a Scotch historian of the Reformation, declares: "It is to Luther that Germany owes its splendid educational system in its roots and in its inception. For he was the first to plead for a universal education—for an education of the whole people, without regard to class or special life work."[3]

On the opposite side are ranged the Catholic writers and some few non-sectarians. Janssen in his elaborate discussion of the "History of the German People" is especially critical of Luther and the effects of his teaching upon the schools. Paulsen shows that the Latin schools were uppermost in Luther's plans, while German was merely used for religious instruction.[4]

This extreme diversity of opinion in regard to Luther's educational and cultural attitudes was not so much due to bigotry or religious prejudice as some might judge. The explanation for it is to be found in his writings as well as in the results which they produced on the school situation in Germany. The diverse and indefinite nature of many of his statements, which were generally made under the heat

[1] *Ibid.*, Preface.
[2] BRUCE, G. M., "Luther as an Educator," p. 299.
[3] LINDSAY, T. M., "Luther and the German Reformation," p. 238.
[4] PAULSEN, F., "German Education," pp. 76–78.

of impulses set off by special and more or less irritating circumstances, is largely responsible.

Luther deals with education directly in many ways; in sermons, tracts, letters, addresses, table talk, commentaries on the Scriptures and other writings. His ideas were a growth. They came as his reactions to the unfolding practical situations which confronted his energetic spirit interested in the reform of life about him. We must recognize also that, even had he never written a line on education, the new religious views which he established had inherent in them a new and vital spirit making for the reform of pedagogy. To insure a clear understanding of his ideas most of the materials presented have been arranged in their chronological order so as to exhibit the development and change in his views. A few passages which have no special time relation are placed together at the end.

First came his vigorous assault upon the church and scholastic philosophy. As part of this primary attack he included the monastic and other schools, the universities, and the methods of family training. In 1520 he wrote the address "To the Christian Nobility of the German Nation Respecting the Reformation of the Christian Estate," in which he urges reform of the universities and suggests elementary schools for boys and girls.

His positive views of religion at this stage are liberal and even radical. Salvation, he holds, is a matter of faith in Christ, and neither the church nor the state has authority over the individual conscience. Everyone is a free agent in

his relations to God. The monasteries and all church benefices must be suppressed; all church authorities, from the
pope down, must be overthrown. Everyone is to live the
simple Christian life of honesty, industry, and righteousness.

Among the first reactions to the new doctrines, we find
that the peasants assumed that the millennium was about
to dawn and all political, social, and economic, as well as
ecclesiastical, oppression come to an end. They believed it
was no longer necessary to study the learned languages, for
the Bible in the vernacular was all-sufficient for every purpose of life. Schools and learning were no longer required,
especially as learning no longer prepared one for appointment to a church living. Support of the church, too, and
sacrifices for charity were no means of grace. In a word,
the first act in the tremendous drama of the Reformation
threatened to produce a general state of chaos. All the older
types of schools and the universities declined, and many
went completely out of existence. To combat this wide-
spread revolt against religion and education, Luther felt
obliged to exert his full energies.

His first step was the "Letter to the Mayors and Aldermen of All the Cities of Germany" in 1524 in which he
urged the establishment of schools and reproved the people
for preferring to send their children to the vernacular
reading-writing schools rather than the Latin schools. He
declared: "Because selfish parents see that they can no
longer place their children upon the bounty of monasteries
and cathedrals, they refuse to educate them. 'Why should

we educate our children,' they say, 'if they are not to become priests, monks, and nuns, and thus earn a support?' " [1] As a second step he urged that everywhere a visitation or survey should be undertaken so as to secure accurate information in regard to church and school conditions. A survey was made in Saxony in 1527 and this was followed by numerous surveys made in other principalities.

A turning point in Luther's experience and attitudes came during the years 1525 to 1528. Three contacts profoundly affected his judgment and altered his views on education. These were the Peasants' War in 1525, the church-school survey in 1527, and the rapid spread of Anabaptist doctrines which followed. After these experiences his views became much more conservative. He revised his views as to the relation of church and state. From now on he conceived religion as the essential factor in the historic culture which makes civilization what it is. Every individual must be brought up in subserviency to the state, and outwardly at least he must be submissive to the religious doctrines and practices of his prince. Schools and universities must be established and conducted by the state. The classical languages must be learned so that direct access may be had to the Scriptures in the original and also to the Church Fathers. Jurists, doctors, preachers, and teachers must be trained for service in their respective spheres.

If the decline of the schools affected him deeply, the Peasa; War in 1525 touched him more profoundly still

[1] S('ow, pp. 47–48.

and altered his attitude toward the peasantry and in regard to the reading of the Scriptures. This change in Luther's attitude can be readily seen in two statements made by him. In 1520 he declared: "We should verily be forced . . . to teach the Holy Scriptures and nothing else." "Should not every Christian be expected by his ninth or tenth year to know all the Gospels, containing as they do his very name and life?" [1] In 1530 he advised instead the use of the catechism and in his "Table Talk" he declared: "The catechism is the right Bible of the laity, wherein is contained the whole sum of Christian doctrine necessary to be known by every Christian to salvation." [2] By this time he questioned the free use of the Scriptures in the hands of the common people.

The dense ignorance, religious defection, and indifference found everywhere in the church-school survey greatly affected Luther. To meet the deplorable need he composed his two catechisms in order to give the masses the elements of religious instruction. Finally, as the supply of pastors and other professional men was scarce and the common people had come to feel a deep distrust of all learning and learned men, in 1530 Luther wrote his famous "Sermon on the Duty of Sending Children to School."

Luther was profoundly interested in the teaching of Latin and Greek, not in order to study the ancient classical authors, whom he regarded as heathenish, but in order to

[1] See below, p. 40.
[2] See below, p. 97.

understand the Scriptures in their purity. He was no humanist, but yet he did more than any one else to establish the Latin schools.

For the common schools as we know them he did little directly. He called upon the authorities to suppress the private vernacular schools which had done much to overcome illiteracy. He subscribed to the Saxon School Order of 1528, which expressly proscribed the teaching of German and Greek.[1] He repeatedly reproved the people for preferring to send their children to the vernacular schools to train them for business rather than to the Latin schools to train them for the ministry and other learned professions.

But Luther the reactionary could not counteract the effects of Luther the reformer. The power of the logic of his early doctrines and of his writings was beyond even his control. Nothing could stop the influence of his German Bible, his catechisms, his hymns and other contributions in making for popular education. In placing education under the control of the state, and advocating compulsory attendance, moreover, he had given it an entirely new status and introduced a factor destined to be the most potent in the evolution of universal education.

No special passage has been selected to explain Luther's views of the relation of the state, church, and school. He treated the relation of the state to the church in a special discussion in 1523, entitled "On Worldly Authority."[2] His

[1] See below, p. 181.
[2] "Von Weltlicher Obrigkeit," "D. Martin Luthers Werke," Weimar ed., Vol. 11, pp. 245–281.

point of view, however, comes out clearly enough in the "Address to the Nobility," the "Letter to the Mayors and Aldermen" and in numerous shorter and more personal letters. As the final outcome of his work the church was subordinate to the state, pastors and teachers became civil officers, and every German was obliged to conform to the religious views of his prince.

CRITICISM OF MONASTIC TRAINING

Translated by Henry Barnard [1]

Solomon was a right royal schoolmaster. He does not forbid children from mingling with the world, or from enjoying themselves, as the monks do their scholars; for they will thus become mere clods and blockheads, as Anselm likewise perceived. Said this one: "A young man, thus hedged about, and cut off from society, is like a young tree, whose nature it is to grow and bear fruit, planted in a small and narrow pot." For the monks have imprisoned the youth whom they have had in charge, as men put birds in dark cages, so that they could neither see nor converse with any one. But it is dangerous for youth to be thus alone, thus debarred from social intercourse. Wherefore, we ought to permit young people to see, and hear, and know what is taking place around them in the world, yet so that you hold

[1] BARNARD, HENRY, "German Teachers and Educators," p. 136, translated from Karl von Raumer, "Geschichte der Pädagogik," Vol. I, p. 114.

them under discipline, and teach them self-respect. Your monkish strictness is never productive of any good fruit. It is an excellent thing for a young man to be frequently in the society of others; yet he must be honorably trained to adhere to the principles of integrity, and to virtue, and to shun the contamination of vice. This monkish tyranny is moreover an absolute injury to the young; for they stand in quite as much need of pleasure and recreation as of eating and drinking; their health, too, will be firmer and the more vigorous by this means.

DUTIES OF PARENTS IN TRAINING CHILDREN

(1519)

Translated by Henry Barnard [1]

Now let us see what parents owe to their children, if they would be parents in the truest sense. St. Paul in Eph. 6: 1,—when commanding children to honor their parents, and setting forth the excellence of this commandment, and its reasonableness, says, "Children, obey your parents in the Lord." Here he intimates that parents should not be such after the flesh merely, as it is with the heathen, but *in the Lord*. And, that children *may* be obedient to their parents in the Lord, he adds this caution to parents, directly afterward in the fourth verse: "And, ye fathers, provoke not

[1] BARNARD, HENRY, "German Teachers and Educators," pp. 132–134, translated from Karl von Raumer, "Geschichte der Pädagogik," Vol. I, pp. 108–111. Original in Georg Walch, "Luthers sämtliche Schriften," Vol. III, pp. 1817–1825.

your children to wrath," lest they be discouraged; "but bring them up in the nurture and admonition of the Lord." The first and foremost care that he here enjoins upon parents with reference to their children, in what pertains to the mind and heart, (for of the nurture of the body he does not speak here at all,) is, that they provoke them not to wrath and discouragement. This is a rebuke to such as display a violent and impetuous temper in the management of their children. For, under such an evil discipline, their disposition, while yet tender and impressible, becomes permanently clouded with fear and diffidence; and so there grows up in their breasts a hatred toward their parents, in so far that they run away from them, and pursue a course that otherwise they never would have entered upon. And, in truth, what hope is there of a child, who exercises hatred and mistrust toward his parents, and is ever downcast in their presence? Nevertheless St. Paul in this passage does not intend to forbid parents altogether from being angry with their children and chastening them; but rather, that they punish them in love, when punishment is necessary; not, as some do, in a passionate spirit, and without bestowing a thought upon their improvement.

A child, who has once become timid, sullen and dejected in spirit, loses all his self-reliance, and becomes utterly unfitted for the duties of life; and fears rise up in his path, so often as any thing comes up for him to do, or to undertake. But this is not all;—for, where such a spirit of fear obtains the mastery over a man in his childhood, he will hardly be able to rid himself of it to the end of his days. For, if children are accustomed to tremble at every word spoken by their father or mother, they will start and quake forever after, even at the rustling of a leaf. Neither should those women, who are employed to attend upon children, ever be allowed to frighten them with their tricks and mummeries, and, above all, never in the night-time. But parents ought much rather to aim at that sort of education for their children, that would inspire them with a wholesome fear; a fear of those things that they ought to fear, and not of those which only make them cowardly, and so inflict a lasting injury upon them. Thus parents go too far to the *left*. Now let us consider how they are led too far to the *right*.

St. Paul teaches, further, that children should be brought up in the nurture and admonition of the Lord; that is, that they should be instructed respecting that which they ought to know, and should be chastised when they do not hold to the doctrine. For instance, they need both that you teach them that which they do not know of God, and also that you punish them when they will not retain this knowledge. Wherefore, see to it, that you cause your children first to be instructed in spiritual things,—that you point them first to God, and, after that, to the world. But in these days, this order, sad to say, is inverted. And it is not to be wondered at; for parents themselves have not learned by their own experience what is this admonition of the Lord, nor do they know much about it from hearsay. Still we had hoped that schoolmasters would remedy this evil,—that in school, at least, children would learn something good, and there have the fear of God implanted in their hearts. But this hope, too, has come to nought. All nations, the Jews especially, keep their children at school more faithfully than Christians. And this is one reason why Christianity is so fallen. For all its hopes of strength and potency are ever committed to the generation that is coming on to the stage; and, if this is neglected in its youth, it fares with Christianity as with a garden that is neglected in the spring time.

For this reason children must be taught the doctrine of God. But this is the doctrine of God, which you must teach your children,—namely, to know our Lord Jesus Christ, to keep ever fresh in their remembrance how he has suffered for our sakes, what he has done, and what commanded. So the children of Israel were commanded of God to show to their children, and to the generation to come, the marvelous things which he did in the sight of their fathers in the land of Egypt.—Ps. 78: 4, 12. And when they have learned all this, but nevertheless do not love God, nor acknowledge their obligations to him in grateful prayer, nor imitate Christ,—then you should lay before them the admonition of the Lord; that is, present to their view the terrible judgments of God, and his anger at the wicked. If a child, from his youth up, learns these things, namely, God's mercies and promises, which will lead him to love God, and his judgments and warnings, which will lead him to fear God,—then, hereafter, when he shall be old, this knowledge will not depart from him.

For God calls upon men to honor him in two ways; namely, to love him as a father, for the benefits which he has rendered, is now rendering, and ever will render toward us; and to fear him as a judge, for the punishments which he has inflicted, and which he will inflict upon the wicked. Hear what he speaks by the mouth of the prophet Malachi, 1:6, "If then I be a father, where is mine honor? And if I be a master, where is my fear?" Therefore, the children of God should learn to sing of mercy and judgment.—Ps. 101:1. And St. Paul intends to convey this two-fold meaning, when he says that children should be brought up in the nurture and admonition of the Lord. It belongs to nurture, to tell your children how God has created all things, and how he has given them their senses, their life, and their soul, and is daily providing them with the good things of his creation. Again, how he has suffered for us all, worked miracles, preached to us, and how he has promised yet greater things. And with all this you should exhort them to be grateful to God, to acknowledge his providence, and to love him as a father. It belongs to admonition, that you tell them how God, aforetime, smote with great plagues the Egyptians, the heathen, the inhabitants of Sodom, the children of Israel, yea, all men in Adam; again, how he is now daily smiting many with pestilence, the sword, the gallows, water, fire, wild beasts, and all manner of diseases, and how he menaces the wicked with future punishment.

This admonition God requires us to make much more prominent to our children than that of men, or human penalties. And this, not without reason; for thus they will be taught always to look out of themselves, and up to God, and to fear not men, but God. For, should they be accustomed to fear their parents alone, it will finally come to pass that, even in respect to things which are pleasing to God, that they will fear the opinions of men, and so will become vacillating and cowardly. On this account children should be educated not only to fear their parents, but to feel that God will be angry with them if they do *not* fear their parents. So will they not be faint-hearted, but courageous, and, should they be deprived of their parents, they will not depart from God, either while good betides them, or when evil days come upon them; for they have learned with the fear of God to fear their parents, and not through their fear of their parents to stand in awe of God.

But what an acceptable sacrifice it is to God, to bring up children thus, we perceive in Gen. 18: 19, where it is said that God could not hide from Abraham what he was about to do, and that, for this reason; "For I know him," God said, "that he will command his children, and they shall keep the way of the Lord." Do you not see that God herein indicates that the knowledge of the doom, which was to come upon Sodom, would prove to the pious Abraham a strong motive to lead him to bring up his children in the fear of the Lord? So Jonadab, a father among the Rechabites, was gloriously extolled and blessed in his children; and that, because he had brought them up in a pious and godly manner, in the fear of the Lord. In such a manner were Tobias, Joachim and Susanna brought up. On the other hand, the judgment pronounced against Eli, because he restrained not his sons, stands forever to warn us in 1 Sam. 3: 13.

EVIL OF LAX DISCIPLINE

(1519)

Translated by Henry Barnard [1]

There is no greater obstacle in the way of Christianity than neglect in the training of the young. If we would reinstate Christianity in its former glory, we must improve and elevate the children, as it was done in the days of old. But, alas! parents are blinded by the delusiveness of natural affection, so that they have come to regard the bodies of their children more than their souls. On this point hear the words of the wise man; Prov. 13: 24.—"He that spareth the rod, hateth his son; but he that loveth him, chasteneth him betimes." Again, 22: 15.—"Foolishness is bound in the heart of a child; but the rod of correction shall drive it far from him." Again, Prov. 23: 14.—"Thou shalt beat him with the rod, and shalt deliver his soul from hell."

BAD METHODS OF TRAINING

(1520)

Translated by Henry Barnard [2]

Are we not fools? See, we have the power to place heaven or hell within reach of our children, and yet we give our-

[1] BARNARD, HENRY, "German Teachers and Educators," p. 135, original in Walch, Vol. X, p. 761. Also Weimar ed., Vol. II, p. 170.

[2] Ibid., p. 134, translated from Karl von Raumer, "Geschichte der Pädagogik," Vol. I, pp. 111–112. Original in Georg Walch, "Luthers sämtliche Schrnten," Vol. III, pp. 1817–1825.

selves no concern about the matter! For what does it profit you, if you are ever so pious for yourself, and yet neglect the education of your children? Some there are, who serve God with an extreme intensity of devotion,—they fast, they wear coarse garments, and are assiduous in such like exercises for themselves; but the true service of God in their families, namely, the training up their children aright,— this they pass blindly by, even as the Jews of old forsook God's temple, and offered sacrifice upon the high places. Whence, it becomes you first to ponder upon what God requires of you, and upon the office that he has laid upon you; as St. Paul spake in 1 Cor. 7: 20.—"Let every man abide in the same calling, wherein he was called." Believe me, it is much more necessary for you to take diligent heed how you may train up your children well, than to purchase indulgences, to make long prayers, to go on pilgrimages to distant shrines, or to impose numerous vows upon yourselves.

Thus, fathers and mothers, ye see, what course it is your duty to adopt toward your children, so that you may be parents indeed, and worthy of the name; wherefore, be circumspect, lest you destroy yourselves, and your children with you. But those destroy their children, who knowingly neglect them, and suffer them to grow up without the nurture and admonition of the Lord; and though they do not themselves set them a bad example, yet they indulge them overmuch, out of an excess of natural affection, and so destroy them. "But," they say, "these are mere children; they neither know nor understand!" That may be; but look at the dog, the horse, or the ass; they have neither reason nor judgment, and yet we train them to follow our bidding, to come or go, to do or to leave undone, at our pleasure. Neither does a block of wood or of stone know whether it will or will not fit into the building, but the master-workman brings it to shape; how much more then a man! Or will you have it that other people's children may be able to learn what is right, but that yours are not? They who are so exceedingly scrupulous and tender, will have their children's sins to bear, precisely as if these sins were their own.

There are others who destroy their children by using foul language and oaths in their presence, or by a corrupt demeanor and example. I have even known some, and, would God there were no more of them, who have sold their daughters or their wives for hire, and made their living thus out of the wages of unchastity. And truly, murderers, beyond all question, do better for their daughters than such parents. There are some who are exceedingly well pleased if their sons betray a fierce and warlike spirit, and are ever ready to give blows, as though it were a great merit in them to show no fear of any one. Such parents are quite likely in the end to pay dear for their folly, and to experience sorrow and anguish, when their sons, as often happens in such cases, are suddenly cut off; nor, in this event, can they justly complain. Again, children are sufficiently inclined to give way to anger and evil passions, and hence it behooves parents to remove temptation from them, as far as possible, by a well-guarded example in themselves, both in words and in actions. For what can the child of a man, whose language is habitually vile and profane, be expected to learn, unless it be the like vileness and profanity?

Others again destroy their children by inducing them to set their affections on the world, by taking no thought for them further than to see that they cultivate graceful manners, dress finely, dance and sing, and all this, to be admired, and to make conquests; for this is the way of the world. In our day, there are but few who are chiefly solicitous to procure their children an abundant supply of those things that pertain to God, and to the interests of the soul; for the most strive to insure them wealth and splendor, honor and pleasure.

Harsh Methods Opposed

(1523)

Translated by Henry Barnard [1]

In commenting on the statement of the Apostle Paul in Gal. 3: 24, "The law was our schoolmaster to bring us unto Christ," Luther deplores flogging and harsh methods of dealing with children. It was not, we may be sure, without allusion to his own experience as a boy, for he relates that he was once flogged fifteen times in a single forenoon.

---

[1] BARNARD, HENRY, "German Teachers and Educators," p. 152. Commentary on the Epistle to the Galatians, "D. Martin Luthers Werke," Weimar ed., Vol. 40, I, p. 529.

It is impossible that a disciple, or a scholar, can love the teacher who is harsh and severe; for, how can he prevail on himself to love one who immures him, as it were, in a dungeon; that is, who constrains him to do that which he will not, and holds him back from doing that which he will; and who, when he does any thing that has been forbidden him, straightway flogs him, and, not content with this, compels him to kiss the rod too. A most gracious and excellent obedience and affection this in the scholar, that comes from an enforced compliance with the harsh orders of a hateful task-master! My friend, do you suppose that he obeys with joy and gladness? But, what does he do when the teacher's back is turned? Does he not snatch up the rod, break it into a thousand pieces, or else throw it into the fire? And, if he had the power, he would not suffer his teacher to whip him again; nay, he would turn the tables on him, and not simply take the rod to him, but cudgel him soundly with a club. Nevertheless, the child needs the discipline of the rod; but it must be tempered with admonition, and directed to his improvement; for, without this, he will never come to any good, but will be ruined, soul and body. . . . A miserable teacher, indeed, would that man be, who should only know how to beat and torment his scholars, without ever being able to teach them any thing. Such schoolmasters there have been, whose schools were nothing but so many dungeons and hells, and themselves tyrants and gaolers; where the poor children were beaten beyond endurance and without cessation, and applied themselves to their task laboriously and with overpushed diligence, but yet with very small profit. . . . A well-informed and faithful teacher, on the other hand, mingles gentle admonition with punishment, and incites his pupils to diligence in their studies, and to a laudable emulation among themselves; and so they become rooted and grounded in all kinds of desirable knowledge, as well as in the proprieties and the virtues of life, and they now do that spontaneously and with delight, which formerly, and under the old discipline, they approached with reluctance and dread.

. . . .

There [1] is that in the nature of young children, which exults, when the reins of discipline are slackened. Nor is the case otherwise with youth, and if they are held in, even with so firm a hand that they cannot break away, nevertheless they will murmur. The right of fathers over their children is derived from God; he is, in truth, the Father of all, "of whom the whole family in heaven and earth is named."—Eph. 3: 15. Wherefore, the authority of earthly fathers over their children should not be exercised in a hard and unfriendly manner. He who governs in anger only adds fuel to the fire. And, if fathers and masters on earth do not acknowledge God, he so orders it that both children and servants shall disappoint their hopes. Experience, too, shows us abundantly, that far more can be accomplished by love, than by slavish fear and constraint.

[1] This passage is taken from Henry Barnard, "German Teachers and Educators," p. 135, translated from Karl von Raumer, "Geschichte der Pädagogik," Vol. I, pp. 112–113. Originals in Georg Walch, "Luthers sämtliche Schriften," Vol. XI, p. 1106.

But it is the duty of children to learn the fear of God first of all; then, to love those who labor for their improvement. The fear of God should never depart from them; for, if they put it away, they become totally unfit to serve God or man. Correction, too, which includes both reproof and chastisement, saves the soul of the child from the endless punishment of hell. Let not the father spare the rod, but let him remember that the work of training up children is an honor which comes from God; yea, if they turn out well, let him give God the glory. Whoso does not know to do this, hates his children and his household, and walks in darkness. For parents, who love their children blindly, and leave them to their own courses, do not better in the end than if they had hated them. And the ruin of children almost invariably lies at the door of parents, and it commonly ensues from one of these two causes; namely, either from undue lenity and foolish fondness, or from unbending severity, and an irritable spirit. Both these extremes are attended with great hazard, and both should be shunned alike.

TO THE CHRISTIAN NOBILITY OF THE GERMAN NATION RESPECTING THE REFORMATION OF THE CHRISTIAN ESTATE

Translated by Wace and Buchheim [1]

The "Address to the Nobility" is Luther's greatest assault upon the papal church and medievalism. The

[1] WACE, HENRY, and C. A. BUCHHEIM, "Luther's Primary Works," pp. 228–234. Original in "D. Martin Luthers Werke," Weimar ed., Vol. 6, pp. 381–469.

passage selected deals only with the reform of the universities and the subjects taught therein. Toward the end he makes a suggestion in regard to schools for boys and also for girls. This address was followed the same year by two other attacks, "Concerning Christian Liberty" and "The Babylonish Captivity of the Church." While these are basic for the Reformation and exhibit its spirit, they contain nothing on education. These three tracts were published in 1520 and represent the conceptions of religious life and education which Luther held at that time.

---

25. The universities also require a good, sound reformation. I must say this, let it vex whom it may. The fact is that whatever the papacy has ordered or instituted is only designed for the propagation of sin and error. What are the universities, as at present ordered, but, as the book of Maccabees says, "schools of 'Greek fashion' and 'heathenish manners' " (Macc. iv 12, 13), full of dissolute living, where very little is taught of the Holy Scriptures and of the Christian faith, and the blind heathen teacher, Aristotle, rules even further than Christ? Now, my advice would be that the books of Aristotle, the "Physics," the "Metaphysics," "Of the Soul," "Ethics," which have hitherto been considered the best, be altogether abolished, with all others that profess to treat of nature, though nothing can be learned from them, either of natural or of spiritual things. Besides, no one has been able to understand his meaning, and much time has been wasted and many noble souls vexed with

much useless labour, study, and expense. I venture to say that any potter has more knowledge of natural things than is to be found in these books. My heart is grieved to see how many of the best Christians this accursed, proud, knavish heathen has fooled and led astray with his false words. God sent him as a plague for our sins.

Does not the wretched man in his best book, "Of the Soul," teach that the soul dies with the body, though many have tried to save him with vain words, as if we had not the Holy Scriptures to teach us fully of all things of which Aristotle had not the slightest perception? Yet this dead heathen has conquered, and has hindered and almost suppressed the books of the living God; so that, when I see all this misery, I cannot but think that the evil spirit has introduced this study.

Then there is the "Ethics," which is accounted one of the best, though no book is more directly contrary to God's will and the Christian virtues. Oh that such books could be kept out of the reach of all Christians! Let no one object that I say too much, or speak without knowledge. My friend, I know of what I speak. I know Aristotle as well as you or men like you. I have read him with more understanding than St. Thomas or Scotus, which I may say without arrogance, and can prove if need be. It matters not that so many great minds have exercised themselves in these matters for many hundred years. Such objections do not affect me as they might have done once, since it is plain as day that many more errors have existed for many hundred years in the world and the universities.

I would, however, gladly consent that Aristotle's books of "Logic," "Rhetoric," and "Poetry" should be retained, or they might be usefully studied in a condensed form, to practise young people in speaking and preaching; but the notes and comments should be abolished, and, just as Cicero's "Rhetoric" is read without note or comment, Aristotle's "Logic" should be read without such long commentaries. But now neither speaking nor preaching is taught out of them, and they are used only for disputation and toilsomeness. Besides this, there are languages,—Latin, Greek, and Hebrew—the mathematics, history; which I recommend to men of higher understanding: and other matters, which will come of themselves, if they seriously strive after reform. And truly it is an important matter, for it concerns the teaching and training of Christian youths and of our noble people, in whom Christianity still abides. Therefore I think that pope and emperor could have no better task than the reformation of the universities, just as there is nothing more devilishly mischievous than an unreformed university.

Physicians I would leave to reform their own faculty; lawyers and theologians I take under my charge, and say firstly that it would be right to abolish the canon law entirely, from the beginning to end, more especially the decretals. We are taught quite sufficiently in the Bible how we ought to act; all this study only prevents the study of the Scriptures, and for the most part it is tainted with covetousness and pride. And even though there were some good in it, it should nevertheless be destroyed, for the Pope having the canon law in *scrinio pectoris*,[1] all further study is useless and deceitful. At the present time the canon law is not to be found in the books, but in the whims of the Pope and his sycophants. You may have settled a matter in the best possible way according to the canon law, but the Pope has his *scrinium pectoris,* to which all law must bow in all the world. Now this *scrinium* is oftentimes directed by some knave and the devil himself, whilst it boasts that it is directed by the Holy Ghost. This is the way they treat Christ's poor people, imposing many laws and keeping none, forcing others to keep them or to free themselves by money.

Therefore, since the Pope and his followers have cancelled the whole canon law, despising it and setting their own will above all the world, we should follow them and reject the books. Why should we study them to no purpose? We should never be able to know the Pope's caprice, which has now become the canon law. Let it fall then in God's name, after having risen in the devil's name. Let there be henceforth no *doctor decretorum,* but let them all be *doctores scrinii papalis,* that is the Pope's sycophants. They say that there is no better temporal government than among the Turks, though they have no canon nor civil law, but only their Koran; we must at least own that there is no worse government than ours, with its canon and civil law, for no estate lives according to the Scriptures, or even according to natural reason.

The civil law, too, good God! what a wilderness it is

[1] In the shrine of his heart.

become! It is indeed, much better, more skilful, and more honest than the canon law, of which nothing is good but the name. Still there is far too much of it. Surely good governors, in addition to the Holy Scriptures, would be law enough, as St. Paul says, "Is it so that there is not a wise man among you, no, not one that shall be able to judge between his brethren?" (1 Cor. vi. 5). I think also that the common law and the usage of the country should be preferred to the law of the empire, and that the law of the empire should only be used in cases of necessity. And would to God that, as each land has its own peculiar character and nature, they could all be governed by their own simple laws, just as they were governed before the law of the empire was devised, and as many are governed even now! Elaborate and far-fetched laws are only burdensome to the people, and a hindrance rather than a help to business. But I hope that others have thought of this, and considered it to more purpose than I could.

Our worthy theologians have saved themselves much trouble and labour by leaving the Bible alone and only reading the "Sentences." [1] I should have thought that young theologians might begin by studying the "Sentences," and that doctors should study the Bible. Now they invert this: The Bible is the first thing they study; this ceases with the Bachelor's degree; the "Sentences" are the last, and these they keep for ever with the Doctor's degrees, and this, too, under

[1] Luther refers here to the "Sentences" of Petrus Lombardus, the so-called *magister sententiarum,* which formed the basis of all dogmatic interpretation from about the middle of the twelfth century down to the Reformation.

such sacred obligation that one that is not a priest may read the Bible, but a priest must read the "Sentences"; so that, as far as I can see, a married man might be a doctor in the Bible, but not in the "Sentences." How should we prosper so long as we act so perversely, and degrade the Bible, the holy word of God? Besides this, the Pope orders with many stringent words that his laws be read and used in schools and courts; while the law of the Gospel is but little considered. The result is that in schools and courts the Gospel lies dusty underneath the benches, so that the Pope's mischievous laws may alone be in force.

Since then we hold the name and title of teachers of the Holy Scriptures, we should verily be forced to act according to our title, and to teach the Holy Scriptures and nothing else. Although, indeed, it is a proud, presumptuous title for a man to proclaim himself teacher of the Scriptures, still it could be suffered, if the works confirmed the title. But as it is, under the rule of the "Sentences," we find among theologians more human and heathenish fallacies than true holy knowledge of the Scriptures. What then are we to do? I know not, except to pray humbly to God to give us Doctors of Theology. Doctors of Arts, of Medicine, of Law, of the "Sentences," may be made by popes, emperors, and the universities; but of this we may be certain: a Doctor of the Holy Scriptures can be made by none but the Holy Ghost, as Christ says, "They shall all be taught of God" (John vi. 45). Now the Holy Ghost does not consider red caps or brown, or any other pomp, nor whether we are young or old, layman or priest, monk or secular, virgin or married; nay, He once spoke by an ass against the prophet that rode on it. Would to God we were worthy of having such doctors given us, be they laymen or priests, married or unmarried! But now they try to force the Holy Ghost to enter into popes, bishops, or doctors, though there is no sign to show that He is in them.

We must also lessen the number of theological books, and choose the best, for it is not the number of books that makes the learned man, nor much reading, but good books often read, however few, make a man learned in the Scriptures and pious. Even the Fathers should only be read for a short time as an introduction to the Scriptures. As it is we read nothing else, and never get from them into the Scriptures, as if one should be gazing at the sign-posts and never follow the road. These good Fathers wished to lead us into the Scriptures by their writings, whereas we lead ourselves out by them, though the Scriptures are our vineyard, in which we should all work and exercise ourselves.

Above all, in schools of all kinds the chief and most common lesson should be the Scriptures, and for young boys the Gospel; and would to God each town had also a girls' school, in which girls might be taught the Gospel for an hour daily, either in German or Latin! In truth, schools, monasteries, and convents were founded for this purpose, and with good Christian intentions, as we read concerning St. Agnes and other saints; then were there holy virgins and martyrs; and in those times it was well with Christendom; but now it has been turned into nothing but prayer and singing. Should not every Christian be expected by his ninth or tenth year to know all the holy Gospels, containing as they do his very name and life? A spinner or a seamstress teaches her daughter her trade while she is young, but now even the most learned prelates and bishops do not know the Gospel.

Oh, how badly we treat all these poor young people that are entrusted to us for discipline and instruction! and a heavy reckoning shall we have to give for it that we keep them from the word of God; their fate is that described by Jeremiah: "Mine eyes do fail with tears, my bowels are troubled, my liver is poured upon the earth, for the destruction of the daughter of my people, because the children and the sucklings swoon in the streets of the city. They say to their mothers, Where is corn and wine? when they swooned as the wounded in the streets of the city, when their soul was poured out into their mother's bosom" (Lam. ii 11, 12). We do not perceive all this misery, how the young folk are being pitifully corrupted in the midst of Christendom, all for want of the Gospel, which we should always read and study with them.

However, even if the High Schools studied the Scriptures diligently we should not send every one to them, as we do now, when nothing is considered but numbers, and every man wishes to have a Doctor's title; we should only send the aptest pupils, well prepared in the lower schools. This should be seen to by princes or the magistrates of the towns, and they should take care none but apt pupils be sent. But where the Holy Scriptures are not the rule, I advise no one to send his child. Everything must perish where God's word is not studied unceasingly; and so we see what manner of men there are now in the High Schools, and all this is the fault of no one but the Pope, the bishops, and the prelates, to whom the welfare of the young has been entrusted. For the High Schools should only train men of good understanding in the Scriptures, who wish to become bishops and priests, and to stand at our head against heretics and the devil and all the world. But where do we find this? I greatly fear the High Schools are nothing but great gates of hell, unless they diligently study the Holy Scriptures and teach them to the young people.

LUTHER AND HUMANISM

Translated by Preserved Smith and Charles M. Jacobs [1]

The intensity of religious and theological interest weakened attention to humanistic study. As we have already seen, Erasmus and others charged Lutheranism with causing the downfall of liberal learning. The chief center of German humanism was the University of Erfurt, and the leading humanistic scholar was Eoban Hess. Luther had been a student at Erfurt but was never identified with the humanistic circle. For, as Beard has well stated, Luther was Hebraic rather than Hellenic in spirit. The following letter is the response

[1] "Luther's Correspondence and Other Contemporary Letters," translated and edited by Preserved Smith, Ph.D., and Charles M. Jacobs, D.D., pp. 176–177. This letter and a number of others by the same translators are reprinted by permission of the United Lutheran Publishing House, Philadelphia, Pa.

of Luther to the despair over the lack of humanistic interest which Hess had expressed in a lengthy poem.

Luther to Eoban Hess.

Wittenberg, March 29, 1523.

. . . Do not be disturbed by the fears, which you express, that our theology will make us Germans more barbarous in letters than ever we have been; some people often have their fears when there is nothing to fear. I am persuaded that without knowledge of literature pure theology cannot at all endure, just as heretofore, when letters have inclined and lain prostrate, theology, too, has wretchedly fallen and lain prostrate; nay, I see that there has never been a great revelation of the Word of God unless He has first prepared the way by the rise and prosperity of languages and letters, as though they were John the Baptists. There is, indeed, nothing that I have less wished to see done against our young people than that they should omit to study poetry and rhetoric. Certainly it is my desire that there shall be as many poets and rhetoricians as possible, because I see that by these studies, as by no other means, people are wonderfully fitted for the grasping of sacred truth and for handling it skillfully and happily. To be sure, "Wisdom maketh the tongues of those who cannot speak eloquent," but the gift of tongues is not to be despised. Therefore I beg of you that at my request (if that has any weight) you will urge your young people to be diligent in the study of poetry and rhetoric. As Christ lives, I am often angry with myself that my

44

age and my manner of life do not leave me any time to busy myself with the poets and orators. I had bought me a Homer that I might become a Greek. . . .

LETTER TO THE MAYORS AND ALDERMEN OF ALL THE CITIES OF GERMANY IN BEHALF OF CHRISTIAN SCHOOLS

Translated by F. V. N. Painter [1]

This lengthy letter was Luther's most important work for education. It was written in 1524, four years after his appeal to the German princes to reform the church. These years were full of turmoil and revolutionizing changes. All the schools, high and low, began to decline. The chief schools had been conducted in the monasteries, the nunneries, and the churches. Luther denounced these institutions most vigorously and was not sorry to see them destroyed. But a new condition arose which threatened to destroy all culture—due to the idea of the common people that it was no longer necessary to learn the ancient languages and the higher studies. The common people held that the Scriptures in the vernacular were all-sufficient. They distrusted the universities and viewed with suspicion the sophistry and pride of higher learning. This letter was the beginning of Luther's efforts to establish a new order

[1] PAINTER, F. V. N., "Luther on Education," pp. 169–209. Dr. Painter used the Leipzig edition of Luther's works; the same letter will be found in the Weimar edition, Vol. 15, pp. 9–53. Reprinted by permission of Concordia Publishing House, St. Louis, Mo.

of education and to show wherein the popular notions were wrong. It was natural that he should appeal to the authorities of the towns and cities. For several centuries in the progressive Hanseatic towns of the North these officials had moved to establish and maintain schools in which the children could learn to read, write, and calculate. While demands for these primary arts had been increasingly expressed by the rising commercial class, the church had all along fought this form of education. Now that Luther had turned from the Catholic Church, he appealed to these city authorities to take over the entire work of education.

———

Grace and Peace from God our Father and the Lord Jesus Christ. HONORED AND DEAR SIRS: Having three years ago been put under the ban and outlawed,[1] I should have kept silent, had I regarded the command of men more than that of God. Many persons in Germany both of high and low estate assail my discourses and writings on that account, and shed much blood over them. But God who has opened my mouth and bidden me speak, stands firmly by me, and without any counsel or effort of mine strengthens and extends my cause the more, the more they rage, and seems, as the second Psalm says, to "have them in derision." By this alone any one not blinded by prejudice may see that the work is of God; for it exhibits the divine method, according to which God's cause spreads most rapidly when men exert themselves most to oppose and suppress it.

[1] This refers to his condemnation at the Diet of Worms.

Therefore, as Isaiah says, I will not hold my peace until the righteousness of Christ go forth as brightness, and his salvation as a lamp that burneth.[1] And I beseech you all, in the name of God and of our neglected youth, kindly to receive my letter and admonition, and give it thoughtful consideration. For whatever I may be in myself, I can boast with a clear conscience before God that I am not seeking my own interest, (which would be best served by silence,) but the interest of all Germany, according to the mission, (doubt it who will,) with which God has honored me. And I wish to declare to you frankly and confidently that if you hear me, you hear not me but Christ; and whoever will not hear me, despise not me but Christ.[2] For I know the truth of what I declare and teach; and every one who rightly considers my doctrine will realize its truth for himself.

First of all we see how the schools are deteriorating throughout Germany. The universities are becoming weak, the monasteries are declining, and, as Isaiah says, "The grass withereth, the flower fadeth, because the spirit of the Lord bloweth upon it,"[3] through the Gospel. For through the word of God the unchristian and sensual character of these institutions is becoming known. And because selfish parents see that they can no longer place their children upon the bounty of monasteries and cathedrals, they refuse to educate them. "Why should we educate our children," they

---

[1] An adaptation of Isa. lxii. 1.
[2] A reference to Luke x. 16.
[3] Isa. xl. 7.

say, "if they are not to become priests, monks, and nuns, and thus earn a support?"

The hollow piety and selfish aims of such persons are sufficiently evident from their own confession. For if they sought anything more than the temporal welfare of their children in monasteries and the priesthood, if they were deeply in earnest to secure the salvation and blessedness of their children, they would not lose interest in education and say, "if the priestly office is abolished, we will not send our children to school." But they would speak after this manner: "if it is true, as the Gospel teaches, that such a calling is dangerous to our children, teach us another way in which they may be pleasing to God and become truly blessed; for we wish to provide not alone for the bodies of our children, but also for their souls." Such would be the language of faithful Christian parents.

It is no wonder that the devil meddles in the matter, and influences groveling hearts to neglect the children and the youth of the country. Who can blame him for it? He is the prince and god of this world,[1] and with extreme displeasure sees the Gospel destroy his nurseries of vice, the monasteries and priesthood, in which he corrupts the young beyond measure, a work upon which his mind is especially bent. How could he consent to a proper training of the young? Truly he would be a fool if he permitted such a thing in his kingdom, and thus consented to its overthrow: which indeed would happen, if the young should escape him, and be brought up to the service of God.

[1] A reference to John xiv. 30.

Hence he acted wisely at the time when Christians were educating and bringing up their children in a Christian way. Inasmuch as the youth of the land would have thus escaped him, and inflicted an irreparable injury upon his kingdom, he went to work and spread his nets, established such monasteries, schools, and orders, that it was not possible for a boy to escape him without the miraculous intervention of God. But now that he sees his snares exposed through the Word of God, he takes an opposite course, and dissuades men from all education whatever. He thus pursues a wise course to maintain his kingdom and win the youth of Germany. And if he secures them, if they grow up under his influence and remain his adherents, who can gain any advantage over him? He retains an easy and peaceful mastery over the world. For any fatal wound to his cause must come through the young, who, brought up in the knowledge of God, spread abroad the truth and instruct others.

Yet no one thinks of this dreadful purpose of the devil, which is being worked out so quietly that it escapes observation; and soon the evil will be so far advanced that we can do nothing to prevent it. People fear the Turks, wars, and floods, for in such matters they can see what is injurious or beneficial; but what the devil has in mind no one sees or fears. Yet where we would give a florin to defend ourselves against the Turks, we should give a hundred florins to protect us against ignorance, even if only one boy could be taught to be a truly Christian man; for the good such a man can accomplish is beyond all computation.

Therefore I beg you all, in the name of God and of our neglected youth, not to think of this subject lightly, as many do who see not what the prince of this world intends. For the right instruction of youth is a matter in which Christ and all the world are concerned. Thereby are we all aided. And consider that great Christian zeal is needed to overcome the silent, secret, and artful machinations of the devil. If we must annually expend large sums on muskets, roads, bridges, dams, and the like, in order that the city may have temporal peace and comfort, why should we not apply as much to our poor, neglected youth, in order that we may have a skillful school-master or two?

There is one consideration that should move every citizen, with devout gratitude to God, to contribute a part of his means to the support of schools—the consideration that if divine grace had not released him from exactions and robbery, he would still have to give large sums of money for indulgences, masses, vigils, endowments, anniversaries, mendicant friars, brotherhoods, and other similar impositions. And let him be sure that where turmoil and strife exist, there the devil is present, who did not writhe and struggle so long as men blindly contributed to convents and masses. For Satan feels that his cause is suffering injury. Let this, then, be the first consideration to move you,—that in this work we are fighting against the devil, the most artful and dangerous enemy of men.

Another consideration is found in the fact that we should not, as St. Paul says, receive the grace of God in vain,[1] and

[1] 2 Cor. vi. 1.

neglect the present favorable time. For Almighty God has truly granted us Germans a gracious visitation, and favored us with a golden opportunity. We now have excellent and learned young men, adorned with every science and art, who, if they were employed, could be of great service as teachers. Is it not well known that a boy can now be so instructed in three years, that at the age of fifteen or eighteen he knows more than all the universities and convents have known heretofore? Yea, what have men learned hitherto in the universities and monasteries, except to be asses and blockheads? Twenty, forty years, it has been necessary to study, and yet one has learned neither Latin nor German! I say nothing of the shameful and vicious life in those institutions, by which our worthy youth have been so lamentably corrupted.

I should prefer, it is true, that our youth be ignorant and dumb rather than that the universities and convents should remain as the only sources of instruction open to them. For it is my earnest intention, prayer and desire that these schools of Satan either be destroyed or changed into Christian schools. But since God has so richly favored us, and given us a great number of persons who are competent thoroughly to instruct and train our young people, it is truly needful that we should not disregard His grace and let Him knock in vain. He stands at the door; happy are we if we open to Him. He calls us; happy is the man who answers Him. If we disregard His call, so that He passes by, who will bring Him back?

Let us consider the wretchedness of our former condition

and the darkness in which we were enveloped. I believe Germany has never heard so much of the Word of God as at the present time; history reveals no similar period. If we let the gracious season pass without gratitude and improvement, it is to be feared that we shall suffer still more terrible darkness and distress. My dear countrymen, buy while the market is at your door; gather the harvest while the sun shines and the weather is fair: use the grace and Word of God while they are near. For know this, that the Word and grace of God are like a passing shower, which does not return where it has once been. The Divine favor once rested upon the Jews, but it has departed. Paul brought the Gospel into Greece; but now they have the Turks. Rome and Italy once enjoyed its blessings; but now they have the Pope. And the German people should not think that they will always have it; for ingratitude and neglect will banish it. Therefore seize it and hold it fast, whoever can; idle hands will have an evil year.

The third consideration is the highest of all, namely, God's command, which through Moses so often urges and enjoins that parents instruct their children, that the seventy-eighth Psalm says: "He established a testimony in Jacob, and appointed a law in Israel, which he commanded our fathers that they should make them known to their children." And the fourth commandment also shows this, where he has so strictly enjoined children to obey their parents, that disobedient children were to be put to death. And why do old people live, except to care for, teach, and bring up the young? It is not possible for inexperienced youth to instruct and care for themselves; and for that reason God has commended them to us who are older and know what is good for them, and He will require a strict account at our hands. Therefore Moses gives this injunction: "Ask thy father, and he will show thee; thy elders, and they will tell thee." [1]

It is indeed a sin and shame that we must be aroused and incited to the duty of educating our children and of considering their highest interests, whereas nature itself should move us thereto, and the example of the heathen affords us varied instruction. There is no irrational animal that does not care for and instruct its young in what they should know, except the ostrich, of which God says: "She leaveth her eggs in the earth, and warmeth them in the dust; and is hardened against her young ones, as though they were not hers." [2] And what would it avail if we possessed and performed all else, and became perfect saints, if we neglect that for which we chiefly live, namely, to care for the young? In my judgment there is no other outward offense that in the sight of God so heavily burdens the world, and deserves such heavy chastisement, as the neglect to educate children.

In my youth this proverb was current in the schools: "It is no less a sin to neglect a pupil than to do violence to a woman." It was used to frighten teachers. But how much lighter is this wrong against a woman (which as a bodily sin may be atoned for), than to neglect and dishonor immortal souls, when such a sin is not recognized and can

[1] Deut. xxxii. 7.
[2] Job xxxix, 14, 15.

53

never be atoned for? O eternal woe to the world! Children are daily born and grow up among us, and there are none, alas! who feel an interest in them; and instead of being trained, they are left to themselves. The convents and cathedral schools are the proper agencies to do it; but to them we may apply the words of Christ: "Woe unto the world because of offenses! Whoso shall offend one of these little ones which believe in me, it were better for him that a mill-stone were hanged about his neck, and that he were drowned in the depths of the sea." [1] They are nothing but destroyers of children.

But all that, you say, is addressed to parents; what does it concern the members of the council and the mayors? That is true; but how, if parents neglect it? Who shall attend to it then? Shall we therefore let it alone, and suffer the children to be neglected? How will the mayors and council excuse themselves, and prove that such a duty does not belong to them?

Parents neglect this duty from various causes.

In the first place, there are some who are so lacking in piety and uprightness that they would not do it if they could, but like the ostrich, harden themselves against their own offspring, and do nothing for them. Nevertheless these children must live among us and with us. How then can reason and, above all, Christian charity, suffer them to grow up ill-bred, and to infect other children, till at last the whole city be destroyed, like Sodom, Gomorrah, and some other cities?

[1] Matt. xviii. 6, 7.

In the second place, the great majority of parents are unqualified for it, and do not understand how children should be brought up and taught. For they have learned nothing but to provide for their bodily wants; and in order to teach and train children thoroughly, a separate class is needed.

In the third place, even if parents were qualified and willing to do it themselves, yet on account of other employ· ments and household duties they have no time for it, so that necessity requires us to have teachers for public schools, unless each parent employ a private instructor. But that would be too expensive for persons of ordinary means, and many a bright boy, on account of poverty, would be neglected. Besides, many parents die and leave orphans; and how they are usually cared for by guardians, we might learn, even if observation were not enough, from the sixty-eighth Psalm, where God calls himself the "Father of the fatherless," as of those who are neglected by all others. Also there are some who have no children and therefore feel no interest in them.

Therefore it will be the duty of the mayors and council to exercise the greatest care over the young. For since the happiness, honor, and life of the city are committed to their hands, they would be held recreant before God and the world, if they did not, day and night, with all their power, seek its welfare and improvement. Now the welfare of a city does not consist alone in great treasures, firm walls, beautiful houses, and munitions of war; indeed, where all these are found, and reckless fools come into power, the city sustains the greater injury. But the highest welfare, safety, and power of a city consists in able, learned, wise, upright, cultivated citizens, who can secure, preserve, and utilize every treasure and advantage.

In ancient Rome the boys were so brought up that at the age of fifteen, eighteen, twenty, they were masters not only of the choicest Latin and Greek, but also of the liberal arts, as they are called; and immediately after this scholastic training, they entered the army or held a position under the government. Thus they became intelligent, wise, and excellent men, skilled in every art and rich in experience, so that all the bishops, priests, and monks in Germany put together would not equal a Roman soldier. Consequently their country prospered; persons were found capable and skilled in every pursuit. Thus, in all the world, even among the heathen, school-masters and teachers have been found necessary where a nation was to be elevated. Hence in the Epistle to the Galatians Paul employs a word in common use when he says, "The law was our *school-master*." [1]

Since, then, a city must have well-trained people, and since the greatest need, lack, and lament is that such are not to be found, we must not wait till they grow up of themselves; neither can they be hewed out of stones nor cut out of wood; nor will God work miracles, so long as men can attain their object through means within their reach. Therefore we must see to it, and spare no trouble or expense to educate and form them ourselves. For whose fault is it that in all the cities there are at present so few skillful people except the rulers, who have allowed the young to grow up like trees in the forest, and have not

[1] Gal. iii. 24.

cared how they were reared and taught? The growth, consequently, has been so irregular that the forest furnishes no timber for building purposes, but like a useless hedge, is good only for fuel.

Yet there must be civil government. For us, then, to permit ignoramuses and blockheads to rule when we can prevent it, is irrational and barbarous. Let us rather make rulers out of swine and wolves, and set them over people who are indifferent to the manner in which they are governed. It is barbarous for men to think thus: "We will now rule; and what does it concern us how those fare who shall come after us?" Not over human beings, but over swine and dogs should such people rule, who think only of their own interests and honor in governing. Even if we exercise the greatest care to educate able, learned and skilled rulers, yet much care and effort are necessary in order to secure prosperity. How can a city prosper, when no effort is made?

But, you say again, if we shall and must have schools, what is the use to teach Latin, Greek, Hebrew, and the other liberal arts? Is it not enough to teach the Scriptures, which are necessary to salvation, in the mother tongue? To which I answer: I know, alas! that we Germans must always remain irrational brutes, as we are deservedly called by surrounding nations. But I wonder why we do not also say: of what use to us are silk, wine, spices, and other foreign articles, since we ourselves have an abundance of wine, corn, wool, flax, wood, and stone in the German states, not only for our necessities, but also for embellishment and ornament? The languages and other liberal arts, which are not only harmless, but even a greater ornament, benefit, and honor than these things, both for understanding the Holy Scriptures and carrying on the civil government, we are disposed to despise; and the foreign articles which are neither necessary nor useful, and which besides greatly impoverish us, we are unwilling to dispense with. Are we not rightly called German dunces and brutes?

Indeed, if the languages were of no practical benefit, we ought still to feel an interest in them as a wonderful gift of God, with which he has now blessed Germany almost beyond all other lands. We do not find many instances in which Satan has fostered them through the universities and cloisters; on the contrary, these institutions have fiercely inveighed and continue to inveigh against them. For the devil scented the danger that would threaten his kingdom, if the languages should be generally studied. But since he could not wholly prevent their cultivation, he aims at least to confine them within such narrow limits, that they will of themselves decline and fall into disuse. They are to him no welcome guest, and consequently he shows them scant courtesy in order that they may not remain long. This malicious trick of Satan is perceived by very few.

Therefore, my beloved countrymen, let us open our eyes, thank God for this precious treasure, and take pains to preserve it, and to frustrate the design of Satan. For we cannot deny that, although the Gospel has come and daily comes through the Holy Spirit, it has come by means of the languages, and through them must increase and be preserved.

For when God wished through the apostles to spread the Gospel abroad in all the world, he gave the languages for that purpose; and by means of the Roman empire he made Latin and Greek the language of many lands, that his Gospel might speedily bear fruit far and wide. He has done the same now. For a time no one understood why God had revived the study of the languages; but now we see that it was for the sake of the Gospel, which he wished to bring to light and thereby expose and destroy the reign of Antichrist. For the same reason he gave Greece a prey to the Turks, in order that Greek scholars, driven from home and scattered abroad, might bear the Greek tongue to other countries, and thereby excite an interest in the study of languages.

In the same measure that the Gospel is dear to us, should we zealously cherish the languages. For God had a purpose in giving the Scriptures only in two languages, the Old Testament in the Hebrew, and the New Testament in the Greek. What God did not despise, but chose before all others for His Word, we should likewise esteem above all others. St. Paul, in the third chapter of Romans, points out, as a special honor and advantage of the Hebrew language, that God's Word was given in it: "What profit is there of circumcision? Much every way; chiefly because that unto them were committed the oracles of God." [1] Likewise King David boasts in the one hundred and forty-seventh Psalm: "He showeth his word unto Jacob, his statutes and his judg-

[1] Rom. iii. 1, 2.

ments unto Israel. He hath not dealt so with any nation: and as for his judgments, they have not known them." [1] Hence the Hebrew language is called sacred. And St. Paul, in Romans i. 2, speaks of the Hebrew Scriptures as holy, no doubt because of the Word of God which they contain. In like manner the Greek language might well be called holy, because it was chosen, in preference to others, as the language of the New Testament. And from this language, as from a fountain, the New Testament has flowed through translations into other languages, and sanctified them also.

And let this be kept in mind, that we will not preserve the Gospel without the languages. The languages are the scabbard in which the Word of God is sheathed. They are the casket in which this jewel is enshrined; the cask in which this wine is kept; the chamber in which this food is stored. And, to borrow a figure from the Gospel itself, they are the baskets in which this bread, and fish, and fragments are preserved. If through neglect we lose the languages (which may God forbid), we will not only lose the Gospel, but it will finally come to pass that we will lose also the ability to speak and write either Latin or German. Of this let us take as proof and warning the miserable and shocking example presented in the universities and cloisters, in which not only the Gospel has been perverted, but also the Latin and German languages have been corrupted, so that the wretched inmates have become like brutes, unable to

[1] Ps. cxlvii. 19, 20.

speak and write German or Latin, and have almost lost
their natural reason.

The apostles considered it necessary to embody the New
Testament in the Greek language, in order, no doubt, that
it might be securely preserved unto us as in a sacred shrine.
For they foresaw what has since taken place, namely, that
when the divine revelation is left to oral tradition, much
disorder and confusion arise from conflicting opinions and
doctrines. And there would be no way to prevent this evil
and to protect the simple-minded, if the New Testament
was not definitely recorded in writing. Therefore, it is evident that where the languages are not preserved, there the
Gospel will become corrupted.

Experience shows this to be true. For immediately after
the age of the apostles, when the languages ceased to be
cultivated, the Gospel, and the true faith, and Christianity
itself, declined more and more, until they were entirely
lost under the Pope. And since the time that the languages
disappeared, not much that is noteworthy and excellent has
been seen in the Church; but through ignorance of the languages very many shocking abominations have arisen. On
the other hand, since the revival of learning, such a light
has been shed abroad, and such important changes have
taken place, that the world is astonished, and must acknowledge that we have the Gospel almost as pure and unadul-
terated as it was in the times of the apostles, and much
purer than it was in the days of St. Jerome and St. Augustine. In a word, since the Holy Ghost, who does nothing

foolish or useless, has often bestowed the gift of tongues, it is our evident duty earnestly to cultivate the languages, now that God has restored them to the world through the revival of learning.

But many of the church fathers, you say, have become saints and have taught without a knowledge of the languages. That is true. But to what do you attribute their frequent misunderstanding of the Scriptures? How often is St. Augustine in error in the Psalms and in other expositions, as well as Hilary, and indeed all those who have undertaken to explain the Scriptures without an acquaintance with the original tongues? And if perchance they have taught correct doctrine, they have not been sure of the application to be made of particular passages. For example, it is truly said that Christ is the Son of God. But what mockery does it seem to adversaries when as proof of that doctrine Psalm cx. 3 is adduced: *"Tecum principium in die virtutis,"* since in the Hebrew no reference is made in that verse to the Deity. When the faith is thus defended with uncertain reasons and proof-texts, does it not seem a disgrace and mockery in the eyes of such adversaries as are acquainted with the Greek and Hebrew? And they are only rendered the more obstinate in their error, and with good ground hold our faith as a human delusion.

What is the reason that our faith is thus brought into disgrace? It is our ignorance of the languages; and the only remedy is a knowledge of them. Was not St. Jerome forced to make a new translation of the Psalms from the Hebrew, because the Jews, when quotations were made from the

Latin version, derided the Christians, affirming that the passages adduced were not found in the original? The comments of all the ancient fathers who, without a knowledge of the languages, have treated of the Scriptures (although they may teach nothing heretical), are still of such a character that the writers often employ uncertain, doubtful, and inappropriate expressions, and grope like a blind man along a wall, so that they often miss the sense of the text and mould it according to their pious fancy, as in the example mentioned in the last paragraph. St. Augustine himself was obliged to confess that the Christian teacher, in addition to Latin, should be acquainted with Hebrew and Greek. Without this knowledge, the expositor will inevitably fall into mistakes; and even when the languages are understood, he will meet with difficulties.

With a simple preacher of the faith it is different from what it is with the expositor of the Scriptures, or prophet, as St. Paul calls him. The former has so many clear passages and texts in translations, that he is able to understand and preach Christ, and lead a holy life. But to explain the Scriptures, to deal with them independently, and oppose heretical interpreters, such a one is too weak without a knowledge of the languages. But we need just such expositors, who will give themselves to the study and interpretation of the Scriptures, and who are able to controvert erroneous doctrines; for a pious life and orthodox teaching are not alone sufficient. Therefore the languages are absolutely necessary, as well as prophets or expositors; but it is not necessary that every Christian or preacher be such a prophet, ac-

cording to the diversity of gifts of which St. Paul speaks in
I Corinthians xii. 8, 9, and in Ephesians iv. 11.

This explains why, since the days of the apostles, the
Scriptures have remained in obscurity, and no reliable and
enduring expositions have anywhere been written. For even
the holy fathers, as we have said, are often in error, and
because they were not versed in the languages, they seldom
agree. St. Bernard was a man of great ability, so that I am
inclined to place him above all other distinguished teachers, whether ancient or modern; but how often he trifles
with the Scriptures, in a spiritual manner to be sure, and
wrests them from their true meaning! For the same reason
the Papists have said that the Scriptures are of obscure and
peculiar import. But they do not perceive that the trouble
lies in ignorance of the languages; but for this, nothing
simpler has ever been spoken than the Word of God. A
Turk must indeed speak unintelligibly to me, although a
Turkish child of seven years understands him, because I
am unacquainted with the language.

Hence it is foolish to attempt to learn the Scriptures
through the comments of the fathers and the study of many
books and glosses. For that purpose we ought to give ourselves to the languages. For the beloved fathers, because they
were not versed in the languages, have often failed, in spite
of their verbose expositions, to give the meaning of the
text. You peruse their writings with great toil; and yet with
a knowledge of the languages you can get the meaning of
Scripture better than they do. For in comparison with the

64

glosses of the fathers, the languages are as sunlight to darkness.

Since, then, it behooves Christians at all times to use the Bible as their only book and to be thoroughly acquainted with it, especially is it a disgrace and sin at the present day not to learn the languages, when God provides every facility, incites us to study, and wishes to have His word known. O how glad the honored fathers would have been, if they could have learned the languages, and had such access to the Holy Scriptures! With what pain and toil they scarcely obtained crumbs, while almost without effort we are able to secure the whole loaf! O how their industry shames our idleness, yea, how severely will God punish our neglect and ingratitude!

St. Paul, in 1 Corinthians xiv. 29,[1] enjoins that there be judgment upon doctrine—a duty that requires a knowledge of the languages. For the preacher or teacher may publicly read the whole Bible as he chooses, right or wrong, if there be no one present to judge whether he does it correctly or not. But if one is to judge, there must be an acquaintance with the languages; otherwise, the judging will be in vain. Hence, although faith and the Gospel may be preached by ordinary ministers without the languages, still such preaching is sluggish and weak, and the people finally become weary, and fall away. But a knowledge of the languages renders it lively and strong, and faith finds itself constantly renewed through rich and varied instruction. In the first

[1] Let the prophets speak two or three, and let the other judge.

65

Psalm the Scriptures liken such study to "a tree planted by the rivers of water, that bringeth forth its fruit in its season; its leaf also shall not wither."

We should not allow ourselves to be deceived because there are some who, while setting little store by the Scriptures, boast of the Spirit. Some also, like the Waldenses, do not regard the languages useful. But, dear friend, whatever such persons may say, I have also been in the Spirit, and have seen more of His power (if it is allowable to boast of one's self), than they will see in a year, however much they may vaunt themselves. I have also been able to accomplish somewhat, while they have remained without influence, and done little more than boast. I know full well that the Spirit does almost everything. Still I should have failed in my work, if the languages had not come to my aid, and made me strong and immovable in the Scriptures. I might without them have been pious, and preached the Gospel in obscurity; but I could not have disturbed the Pope, his adherents, and all the reign of Antichrist. The devil cares less for the Spirit within me than for my pen and linguistic knowledge. For while the Spirit takes nothing but myself away from him, the Holy Scriptures and the languages drive him from the world and break up his kingdom.

I can not praise the Waldenses for depreciating the languages. For although they taught no heresies, yet they often necessarily failed in their proof-texts, and remained unqualified and unskilled to contend against error for the true faith. Besides, their teaching is so unenlightened, and presented in such peculiar forms, not following the language of Scripture, that I fear it will not continue pure. For it is dangerous to speak of divine things in a manner or in words different from those employed in the Scriptures. In brief, they may lead holy lives and teach among themselves; but because they are without the languages, they will lack what others have lacked, namely, an assured and thorough handling of the Scriptures, and the ability to be useful to other nations. And because they could have done this, and would not, they will have an account to render before God for their neglect.

So much for the utility and necessity of the languages, and of Christian schools for our spiritual interests and the salvation of the soul. Let us now consider the body and inquire: though there were no soul, nor heaven, nor hell, but only the civil government, would not this require good schools and learned men more than do our spiritual interests? Hitherto the Papists have taken no interest in civil government, and have conducted the schools so entirely in the interests of the priesthood, that it has become a matter of reproach for a learned man to marry, and he has been forced to hear remarks like this: "Behold, he has become a man of the world, and cares nothing for the clerical state," just as if the priestly order were alone acceptable to God, and the secular classes, as they are called, belong to Satan, and were unchristian. But in the sight of God, the former rather belong to Satan, while the despised masses (as happened to the people of Israel in the Babylonian captivity) remain in the land and in right relations with God.

It is not necessary to say here that civil government is a

divine institution; of that I have elsewhere said so much, that I hope no one has any doubts on the subject. The question is, how are we to get able and skillful rulers? And here we are put to shame by the heathen, who in ancient times, especially the Greeks and Romans, without knowing that civil government is a divine ordinance, yet instructed the boys and girls with such earnestness and industry that, when I think of it, I am ashamed of Christians, and especially of our Germans, who are such blockheads and brutes that they can say: "Pray, what is the use of schools, if one is not to become a priest?" Yet we know or ought to know, how necessary and useful a thing it is, and how acceptable to God, when a prince, lord, counselor, or other ruler, is well-trained and skillful in discharging, in a Christian way, the functions of his office.

Even if there were no soul, (as I have already said,) and men did not need schools and the languages for the sake of Christianity and the Scriptures, still, for the establishment of the best schools everywhere, both for boys and girls, this consideration is of itself sufficient, namely, that society, for the maintenance of civil order and the proper regulation of the household, needs accomplished and well-trained men and women. Now such men are to come from boys, and such women from girls; hence it is necessary that boys and girls be properly taught and brought up. As I have before said, the ordinary man is not qualified for this task, and can not, and will not do it. Princes and lords ought to do it; but they spend their time in pleasure-driving, drinking, and folly, and are burdened with the weighty duties of the cellar, kitchen, and bedchamber. And though some would be glad to do it, they must stand in fear of the rest, lest they be taken for fools or heretics. Therefore, honored members of the city councils, this work must remain in your hands; you have more time and better opportunity for it than princes and lords.

But each one, you say, may educate and discipline his own sons and daughters. To which I reply: We see indeed how it goes with this teaching and training. And where it is carried to the highest point, and is attended with success, it results in nothing more than that the learners, in some measure, acquire a forced external propriety of manner; in other respects they remain dunces, knowing nothing, and incapable of giving aid or advice. But were they instructed in schools or elsewhere by thoroughly qualified male or female teachers, who taught the languages, other arts, and history, then the pupils would hear the history and maxims of the world, and see how things went with each city, kingdom, prince, man, and woman; and thus, in a short time, they would be able to comprehend, as in a mirror, the character, life, counsels, undertakings, successes, and failures, of the whole world from the beginning. From this knowledge they could regulate their views, and order their course of life in the fear of God, having become wise in judging what is to be sought and what avoided in this outward life, and capable of advising and directing others. But the training which is given at home is expected to make us wise through our own experience. Before that can take place, we shall die a hundred times, and all through life act injudiciously; for much time is needed to give experience.

Now since the young must leap and jump, or have something to do, because they have a natural desire for it which should not be restrained, (for it is not well to check them in everything,) why should we not provide for them such schools, and lay before them such studies? By the gracious arrangement of God, children take delight in acquiring knowledge, whether languages, mathematics, or history. And our schools are no longer a hell or purgatory, in which children are tortured over cases and tenses, and in which with much flogging, trembling, anguish and wretchedness they learn nothing. If we take so much time and pains to teach our children to play cards, sing, and dance, why should we not take as much time to teach them reading and other branches of knowledge, while they are young and at leisure, are quick at learning, and take delight in it? As for myself,[1] if I had children and were able I would have them learn not only the languages and history, but also singing, instrumental music, and the whole course of mathematics. For what is all this but mere child's play, in which the Greeks in former ages trained their children, and by this means became wonderfully skillful people, capable for every undertaking? How I regret that I did not read more poetry and history, and that no one taught me in these branches. Instead of these I was obliged with great cost, labor, and injury, to read Satanic filth, the Aristotelian and Scholastic

[1] Luther was not yet married.

70

philosophy, so that I have enough to do to get rid of it.

But you say, who can do without his children and bring them up, in this manner, to be young gentlemen? I reply: it is not my idea that we should establish schools as they have been heretofore, where a boy has studied Donatus and Alexander [1] twenty or thirty years, and yet has learned nothing. The world has changed, and things go differently. My idea is that boys should spend an hour or two a day in school, and the rest of the time work at home, learn some trade and do whatever is desired, so that study and work may go on together, while the children are young and can attend to both. They now spend tenfold as much time in shooting with cross-bows, playing ball, running, and tumbling about.

In like manner, a girl has time to go to school an hour a day, and yet attend to her work at home; for she sleeps, dances, and plays away more than that. The real difficulty is found alone in the absence of an earnest desire to educate the young, and to aid and benefit mankind with accomplished citizens. The devil much prefers blockheads and drones, that men may have more abundant trials and sorrows in the world.

But the brightest pupils, who give promise of becoming accomplished teachers, preachers, and workers, should be kept longer at school, or set apart wholly for study, as we read of the holy martyrs, who brought up St. Agnes, St.

[1] Donatus wrote a Latin grammar used as a textbook during the middle ages. Alexander was the author of a rhymed Latin grammar of a more advanced character.

Agatha, St. Lucian, and others. For this purpose also the cloisters and cathedral schools were founded, but they have been perverted into another and accursed use. There is great need for such instruction; for the tonsured crowd is rapidly decreasing, and besides, for the most part, the monks are unskilled to teach and rule, since they know nothing but to care for their stomachs, the only thing they have been taught. Hence we must have persons qualified to dispense the Word of God and the Sacraments, and to be pastors of the people. But where will we obtain them, if schools are not established on a more Christian basis, since those hitherto maintained, even if they do not go down, can produce nothing but depraved and dangerous corrupters of youth?

There is consequently an urgent necessity, not only for the sake of the young, but also for the maintenance of Christianity and of civil government, that this matter be immediately and earnestly taken hold of, lest afterwards, although we would gladly attend to it, we shall find it impossible to do so, and be obliged to feel in vain the pangs of remorse forever. For God is now graciously present, and offers his aid. If we despise it, we already have our condemnation with the people of Israel, of whom Isaiah says: "I have spread out my hands all the day unto a rebellious people." [1] And Proverbs i. 24–26: "I have stretched out my hand, and no man regarded: but ye have set at naught all my counsel, and would none of my reproof: I also will laugh at your calamity; I will mock when your fear

[1] Isa. lxv. 2.

cometh." Let us then take heed. Consider for example what great zeal Solomon manifested; for he was so much interested in the young that he took time, in the midst of his imperial duties, to write a book for them called Proverbs. And think how Christ himself took the little children in His arms! How earnestly He commends them to us, and speaks of their guardian angels,[1] in order that He may show us how great a service it is, when we rightly bring them up: on the other hand, how His anger kindles, if we offend the little ones, and let them perish.

Therefore, dear Sirs, take to heart this work, which God so urgently requires at your hands, which pertains to your office, which is necessary for the young, and which neither the world nor the Spirit can do without. We have, alas! lived and degenerated long enough in darkness; we have remained German brutes too long. Let us use our reason, that God may observe in us gratitude for His mercies, and that other lands may see that we are human beings, capable both of learning and of teaching, in order that through us, also, the world may be made better. I have done my part; I have desired to benefit the German states, although some have despised me and set my counsel at naught as knowing better themselves,—to all which I must submit. I know indeed that others could have accomplished it better; but because they were silent, I have done the best I could. It is better to have spoken, even though imperfectly, than to have remained silent. And I have hope that God will rouse some of you to listen to my counsel, and that instead of consider-

[1] Matt. xviii. 10.

ing the adviser, you will let yourselves be moved by the great interests at stake.

Finally, this must be taken into consideration by all who earnestly desire to see such schools established and the languages preserved in the German states; that no cost nor pains should be spared to procure good libraries in suitable buildings, especially in the large cities, which are able to afford it. For if a knowledge of the Gospel and of every kind of learning is to be preserved, it must be embodied in books, as the prophets and apostles did, as I have already shown. This should be done, not only that our spiritual and civil leaders may have something to read and study, but also that good books may not be lost, and that the arts and languages may be preserved, with which God has graciously favored us. St. Paul was diligent in this matter, since he lays the injunction upon Timothy: "Give attendance to reading"; [1] and directs him to bring the books, but especially the parchments left at Troas. [2]

All the kingdoms that have been distinguished in the world have bestowèd care upon this matter, and particularly the Israelites, among whom Moses was the first to begin the work, who commanded them to preserve the book of the law in the ark of God, and put it under the care of the Levites, that any one might procure copies from them. He even commanded the king to make a copy of this book in the hands of the Levites. Among other duties, God directed the Levitical priesthood to preserve and attend to the books.

[1] 1 Tim. iv. 13.
[2] 2 Tim. iv. 13.

74

Afterwards Joshua increased and improved this library, as did subsequently Samuel, David, Solomon, Isaiah, and many kings and prophets. Hence have come to us the Holy Scriptures of the Old Testament, which would not otherwise have been collected and preserved, if God had not required such diligence in regard to it.

After this example the collegiate churches and convents formerly founded libraries, although with few good books. And the injury resulting from the neglect to procure books and good libraries, when there were men and books enough for that purpose, was afterwards perceived in the decline of every kind of knowledge; and instead of good books, the senseless, useless, and hurtful books of the monks, the Catholicon, Florista, Graecista, Labyrinthus, Dormi Secure,[1] and the like were introduced by Satan, so that the Latin language was corrupted, and neither good schools, good instruction, nor good methods of study remained. And as we see, the languages and arts are, in an imperfect manner, recovered from fragments of old books rescued from the worms and dust; and every day men are seeking these literary remains, as people dig in the ashes of a ruined city after treasures and jewels.

Therein we have received our just due, and God has well recompensed our ingratitude, in that we did not consider His benefits, and lay up a supply of good literature when we had time and opportunity, but neglected it, as if we were not concerned. He in turn, instead of the Holy Scriptures and good books, suffered Aristotle and numberless pernicious

[1] Names of Latin grammars and collections of sermons.

75

books to come into use, which only led us further from the Bible. To these were added the progeny of Satan, the monks and the phantoms of the universities, which we founded at incredible cost, and many doctors, preachers, teachers, priests and monks, that is to say, great, coarse, fat asses, adorned with red and brown caps, like swine led with a golden chain and decorated with pearls; and we have burdened ourselves with them, who have taught us nothing useful, but have made us more and more blind and stupid, and as a reward have consumed all our property, and filled all the cloisters, and indeed every corner, with the dregs and filth of their unclean and noxious books, of which we can not think without horror.

Has it not been a grievous misfortune that a boy has hitherto been obliged to study twenty years or longer, in order to learn enough miserable Latin to become a priest and to read the mass? And whoever has succeeded in this, has been called blessed, and blessed the mother that has borne such a child! And yet he has remained a poor ignorant man all through life, and has been of no real service whatever. Everywhere we have had such teachers and masters, who have known nothing themselves, who have been able to teach nothing useful, and who have been ignorant even of the right methods of learning and teaching. How has it come about? No books have been accessible but the senseless trash of the monks and sophists. How could the pupils and teachers differ from the books they studied? A jackdaw does not hatch a dove, nor a fool make a man wise. That is the recompense of our ingratitude, in that we did not use diligence in the formation of libraries, but allowed good books to perish, and bad ones to survive.

But my advice is, not to collect all sorts of books indiscriminately, thinking only of getting a vast number together. I would have discrimination used, because it is not necessary to collect the commentaries of all the jurists, the productions of all the theologians, the discussions of all the philosophers, and the sermons of all the monks. Such trash I would reject altogether, and provide my library only with useful books; and in making the selection, I would advise with learned men.

In the first place, a library should contain the Holy Scriptures in Latin, Greek, Hebrew, German, and other languages. Then the best and most ancient commentators in Greek, Hebrew, and Latin.

Secondly, such books as are useful in acquiring the languages, as the poets and orators, without considering whether they are heathen or Christian, Greek or Latin. For it is from such works that grammar must be learned.

Thirdly, books treating of all the arts and sciences.

Lastly, books on jurisprudence and medicine, though here discrimination is necessary.

A prominent place should be given to chronicles and histories, in whatever languages they may be obtained; for they are wonderfully useful in understanding and regulating the course of the world, and in disclosing the marvelous works of God. O how many noble deeds and wise maxims produced on German soil have been forgotten and lost, because no one at the time wrote them down; or if they were written, no one preserved the books: hence we Germans are unknown in other lands, and are called brutes that know only how to fight, eat, and drink. But the Greeks and Romans, and even the Hebrews, have recorded their history with such particularity, that even if a woman or child did any thing noteworthy, all the world was obliged to read and know it; but we Germans are always Germans, and will remain Germans.

Since God has so graciously and abundantly provided us with art, scholars, and books, it is time for us to reap the harvest and gather for future use the treasures of these golden years. For it is to be feared, (and even now it is beginning to take place,) that new and different books will be produced, until at last, through the agency of the devil, the good books which are being printed will be crowded out by the multitude of ill-considered, senseless, and noxious works. For Satan certainly designs that we should torture ourselves again with Catholicons, Floristas, Modernists, and other trash of the accursed monks and sophists, always learning, yet never acquiring knowledge.

Therefore, my dear Sirs, I beg you to let my labor bear fruit with you. And though there be some who think me too insignificant to follow my advice, or who look down upon me as one condemned by tyrants: still let them consider that I am not seeking my own interest, but that of all Germany. And even if I were a fool, and should yet hit upon something good, no wise man should think it a disgrace to follow me. And even if I were a Turk and heathen, and it should yet appear that my advice was advantageous, not for myself, but for Christianity, no reasonable person would despise my counsel. Sometimes a fool has given better advice than a whole company of wise men. Moses received instruction from Jethro.

Herewith I commend you all to the grace of God. May He soften your hearts, and kindle therein a deep interest in behalf of the poor, wretched, and neglected youth; and through the blessing of God may you so counsel and aid them as to attain to a happy Christian social order in' respect to both body and soul, with all fullness and abounding plenty, to the praise and honor of God the Father, through Jesus Christ our Saviour. Amen.

Wittenberg, 1524.

FAMILY GOVERNMENT THE FOUNDATION OF ALL GOVERNMENT

(1525)

Translated by Henry Barnard [1]

We have now explained, at sufficient length, *how* father and mother are to be honored, and what this commandment includes and teaches, and have shown of what vast consequence it is in the sight of God, that this obedience

[1] BARNARD, HENRY, "German Teachers and Educators," pp. 131–132; "Exposition of the Fourth Commandment." Original in "D. Martin Luthers Werke," Weimar ed., Vol. 16, pp. 500–501.

toward father and mother should become universal. Where this is not the case, you will find neither good manners nor a good government. For, where obedience is not maintained at the fire-side, no power on earth can insure to the city, territory, principality, or kingdom the blessings of a good government; and it is there that all governments and dominions originate. If now the root is corrupt, it is in vain that you look for a sound tree, or for good fruit.

For what is a city, but an assemblage of households? How then is a whole city to be wisely governed, when there is no subordination in its several households, yea, when neither child, maid-servant, nor man-servant submit to authority? Again, a territory: what is it, other than an assemblage of cities, market-towns and villages? Where, now, the households are lawless or mis-governed, how can the whole territory be well-governed? yea, nothing else will appear, from one end of it to the other, but tyranny, witchcraft, murders, robberies and disobedience to every law. Now, a principality is a group of territories, or counties; a kingdom, a group of principalities; and an empire, a group of kingdoms. Thus, the whole wide organization of an empire is all woven out of single households. Wherever, then, fathers and mothers slacken the reins of family government, and leave children to follow their own headstrong courses, there it is impossible for either city, market-town or village, either territory, principality, kingdom, or empire, to enjoy the fruits of a wise and peaceful government. For the son, when grown up, becomes a father, a judge, a mayor, a prince, a king, an emperor, a preacher, a schoolmaster, etc. And, if he has been brought up without restraint, then will the subjects become like their ruler, the members like their head.

For this cause, God has established it as a matter of irrevocable necessity, that men should by all means rule over their own households. For where family government is well-ordered and judicious, all other forms of government go on prosperously. And the reason is, as we have seen, that the whole human race proceeds from the family. For it has pleased God so to ordain, from the beginning, that from father and mother, all mankind should forever derive their being.

Importance of Teaching

Translated by Preserved Smith and Charles M. Jacobs [1]

Luther to Duke John Frederic of Electoral Saxony.

Wittenberg, May 20, 1525.

I have written your Grace's father and lord, my gracious Lord, that he shall set the university in order and secure a man who will undertake the task.

.   .   .   .

Necessity therefore demands that if we are to continue to have a university here, we must take prompt action. It were a pity if such a school, from which the Gospel has gone out into all the world, were to go down, and if, when men are

---

[1] "Luther's Correspondence and Other Contemporary Letters," translated and edited by Preserved Smith, Ph.D., and Charles M. Jacobs, D.D., p. 317.

needed everywhere, nothing were done to educate them. If, then, your Grace is willing to do something, it is my humble request that he will help this cause along and close his ears when certain court-sponges speak contemptuously of writers. For your Grace sees that the world cannot now be ruled by force alone, but must have men of learning, who by preaching and teaching the Word of God, help to restrain the people. If there were no preachers and teachers the temporal government would not long endure, not to speak of the Kingdom of God, which would be taken from us. I hope that in this matter your Grace will show himself gracious and a true Christian. God have your Grace in His keeping.

Your Grace's humble servant.　　　　MART. LUTHER.

A CHURCH, SCHOOL, AND CITY GOVERNMENT SURVEY RECOMMENDED

Translated by Preserved Smith and Charles M. Jacobs [1]

When Luther became aware in the years following the break with Rome that the churches and schools were falling into a state of decline, he began to suggest a visit of inquiry throughout the German states. He had this in mind as early as 1525.

Luther to the Elector John of Saxony.

Wittenberg, October 31, 1525.

. . . Therefore, gracious Lord, now that the university is

[1] "Luther's Correspondence and Other Contemporary Letters," translated and edited by Preserved Smith, Ph.D., and Charles M. Jacobs, D.D., pp. 341–343.

set in order, and the Order of Worship has been composed and is about to go into use, there remain two things which demand the attention and disposition of your Grace, as our temporal lord. The first thing is that the parishes everywhere are in such miserable condition. No one gives anything or pays for anything; the mass-fees are abolished, and either there are no taxes at all, or else they are too small; the common man does not think of the priests and preachers, and unless your Grace makes a strict law and undertakes to give proper support to the parishes and preaching places, there will soon be no parsonages or schools or pupils, and thus God's Word and Christian worship will be destroyed. Therefore I wish your Grace to let God use him still further and be his faithful tool, to the greater comforting of even your Grace's own conscience; for this is asked of him and required of him by us and by the necessities of the case, and assured by God Himself. Your Grace will find the means to do it. There are enough monasteries, foundations, benefices, charitable endowments and the like if only your Grace will interest himself sufficiently to command that they be inspected, reckoned up and organized. God will give his blessing to this work and prosper it, so that, if God will, the ordinances that concern men's souls will not be hindered by the needs or the neglect of the poor stomach. For this we beseech His divine grace. Amen.

The second thing is a matter of which I once spoke with your Grace here at Wittenberg. Your Grace ought to order an inspection of the temporal government also, and ascertain how the city councils and all other officials conduct their government and preside over the common weal.

Luther to the Elector John of Saxony.[1]

Wittenberg, November 22, 1526.

Grace and peace in Christ. SERENE, HIGHBORN PRINCE, GRACIOUS LORD. For a long time I have brought no supplication to your Grace, and they have now accumulated. I hope your Grace will be patient. There is nothing else for me to do.

In the first place, gracious Lord, the complaints of the pastors almost everywhere are immeasurably great. The peasants will simply not give any more, and so great is this ingratitude for God's holy Word among the people that beyond all doubt God has a great plague in store for us. If I knew how to do it with a good conscience I would even help to bring it about that they should have no pastors or preachers and live like swine, as, indeed, they do. There is no fear of God and no discipline any longer, for the papal ban is abolished and everyone does what he will.

But because all of us, and especially the rulers, are commanded to care for the poor children who are born every day and are growing up, and to keep them in the fear of God and under discipline, we must have schools and pastors and preachers. If the older people do not want them, they may go to the devil; but if the young people are neglected and are not trained, it is the fault of the rulers, and the land will be filled with wild, loose-living people. Thus

[1] *Ibid.,* pp. 383–384.

not only God's command, but our own necessity compels us to find some way out of the difficulty.

But now the enforced rule of the Pope and the clergy is at an end in your Grace's dominions, and all the monasteries and foundations fall into your Grace's hands as the ruler, the duty and the difficulty of setting these things in order comes with them. No one assumes it, or can or ought assume it. Therefore, as I have said to your Grace's chancellor, and to Nicholas von Ende, it will be necessary for your Grace, as the person whom God has called to this work and entrusted with the remedy, to have the land visited as quickly as possible by four persons; two whose specialty is taxes and property, and two who are competent to pass on doctrine and character. These men, at your Grace's command, ought to have the schools and parishes set in order and provided for, where it is necessary.

If there is a town or a village which can do it, your Grace has the power to compel it to support schools, preaching places and parishes. If they are unwilling to do this or to consider it for their own salvation's sake, then your Grace is the supreme guardian of the youth and of all who need his guardianship, and ought to hold them to it by force, so that they must do it. It is just like compelling them by force to contribute and to work for the building of bridges and roads, or any other of the country's needs.

What the country needs and must have ought to be given and helped along by those who use and enjoy the country. Now there is no more necessary thing than the education of the people who are to come after us and be the rulers. But if they cannot do it and are overburdened with other things, there are the monastic properties which were established chiefly for the purpose of relieving the common man, and ought still be used for that purpose.

Your Grace can easily think that in the end there would be an evil rumor, and one that could not be answered, if the schools and the parishes went down and the nobles were to appropriate the monastic properties for themselves. This charge is already made, and some of them are doing it. Since then these properties are of no benefit to your Grace's treasury, and were given in the first place for purposes of worship, they ought rightly to serve this purpose first of all. What remains over your Grace can apply to the country's needs, or give to the poor.

LUTHER'S CATECHISMS

Translated by Henry Wace and C. A. Buchheim [1]

In 1527 and 1528 Luther himself took part in the survey of church and school conditions by visiting some of the parishes. The deplorable ignorance and spiritual indifference which he observed profoundly shocked him. To meet this situation he prepared in 1529 a shorter and a larger catechism. Only the preface and several short excerpts of the shorter catechism can be included to indicate something of the matter and

[1] WACE, HENRY, and C. A. BUCHHEIM, "Luther's Primary Works," pp. 1–5.

form. It will be well to compare this with Calvin's catechism.[1]

The educational value of these catechisms can hardly be overestimated. The teaching of catechisms had been long a practice of the Catholic Church. All the Protestant bodies likewise resorted to this method of instruction. Luther composed the catechisms for the purpose of making them the textbooks for the instruction of all children and ignorant adults. In his great enthusiasm for the Scriptures during his earlier years he wished the Bible to be the only book used. His contact later with the Peasants' War and the teachings of the Anabaptists made him distrustful of the free use of the Scriptures by the common people. Under this conviction he threw all emphasis upon the teaching of the catechism. Many of the church ordinances in Germany of the latter half of the century required the catechism to be taught to children on Sunday afternoon and one afternoon during the week. Numerous translations of these catechisms have been issued in the English-speaking world.

ENCHIRIDION

A Short Catechism for the Use of Ordinary Pastors and Preachers

PREFACE

Martin Luther to all faithful, pious pastors and preachers: Grace, mercy, and peace in Jesus Christ our Lord.

[1] See below, pp. 246–250.

In setting forth this Catechism or Christian doctrine in such a simple, concise, and easy form, I have been compelled and driven by the wretched and lamentable state of affairs which I discovered lately when I acted as inspector. Merciful God, what misery I have seen, the common people knowing nothing at all of Christian doctrine, especially in the villages! and unfortunately many pastors are well-nigh unskilled and incapable of teaching; and though all are called Christians and partake of the Holy Sacrament, they know neither the Lord's Prayer, nor the Creed, nor the Ten Commandments, but live like the poor cattle and senseless swine, though, now that the Gospel is come, they have learnt well enough how they may abuse their liberty.

O ye bishops, how will ye ever answer for it to Christ that ye have so shamefully neglected the people, and have not attended for an instant to your office? May all evil be averted from you! Ye forbid the taking of the Sacrament in one kind, and insist on your human laws, but never inquire whether they know the Lord's Prayer, the Belief, the Ten Commandments, or any of the words of God. Oh, woe upon you for evermore!

Therefore I pray you for God's sake, my good masters and brethren who are pastors or preachers, to attend to your office with all your heart, to take pity on your people, who are commended to your charge, and to help us to introduce the Catechism among the people, especially among the young; and let those who cannot do better take these tables and forms, and instruct the people in them word for word; in this wise:—

First, the preacher must above all things beware of and avoid the use of various and different texts and forms of the Commandments, Lord's Prayer, Belief, Sacrament, etc.; he must take one form and keep to it, and constantly teach the same, year after year. For the young and simple folk must be taught one definite text and version, else they will easily become confused, if to-day we teach thus and next year thus, as though we wanted to improve it, and so all our labour and toil is lost.

This was clearly seen by the worthy fathers, who used the Lord's Prayer, the Belief, the Ten Commandments, all in one form. Therefore we must always teach the young and simple folk in such a manner that we do not alter one syllable, or preach to-morrow differently from to-day.

Therefore choose whatever form thou wilt, and ever keep to it. But if thou preachest to scholars or wise men, thou mayest show thy skill, and vary these articles, and twist them as subtly as thou canst. But with the young keep always to one form, and teach them first of all these articles, namely, the Ten Commandments, the Belief, the Lord's Prayer, etc., according to the text, word for word, so that they may repeat them and learn them by heart.

But as for those who will not learn, let them be told that they deny Christ and are no Christians, and let them not be admitted to the Sacrament, be sponsors to any child, or enjoy any of the liberty of Christians, but be handed over simply to the Pope and his officers, yea, to the devil himself. Besides this, let their parents or masters refuse them food and drink, and tell them that the prince will have such rude people driven from the land.

For though we cannot and may not force any to believe, yet we must train and urge the multitude so that they may know what is right and wrong among those with whom they have their dwelling, food, and life. For whoever would dwell in a town must know and keep the law of which he would enjoy the privileges, whether he believe it, or be a rogue and good-for-nothing in his heart.

Secondly, when they know the text well, teach them next to understand it, so that they know what it means, and take once more the method of these tables, this or some other short method, whichever thou wilt, and keep to it, and do not alter one syllable, just as we said of the text, and take time and leisure over it. For it is not necessary to expound all at once, but one thing after the other. When they understand the First Commandment well, then take the Second, and so on, else they will be overwhelmed and retain none.

Thirdly, now when thou hast taught them this short Catechism, then take the larger Catechism, and give them a deeper and fuller explanation. Explain every commandment, petition, and article, with its various works and uses, its dangers and abuses, as thou wilt find them in abundance in the many little books written about them. And especially dwell on that commandment that is most neglected among thy people. For example, the Seventh [1] Commandment, about stealing, must be vehemently urged among artisans,

[1] *I. e.,* the eighth, as we number them; and so, the fourth, presently mentioned, is our fifth.

tradesmen, and also among peasants and servants, for among such people there is all manner of unfaithfulness and thieving. Again, the Fourth Commandment must be specially urged upon children and the common people, that they may be quiet, faithful, obedient, peaceful; and thou must always adduce many examples from the Bible of how God punished or blessed such people.

Especially urge authorities and parents that they govern well and send the children to school, and admonish them how it is their duty to do this, and what an accursed sin they commit if they neglect it. For thereby they overthrow and desolate both God's kingdom and the world's, as the worst enemies both of God and man. Lay also great stress on the horrible injury they do, if they do not help to train children for pastors, preachers, clerks, etc., and that God will punish them terribly. For it is very necessary to preach on this subject. Parents and magistrates now sin in this matter more than we can say. The devil has also most evil designs therein.

Finally, because the tyranny of the Pope is past, they will no longer come to the Sacrament, and despise it. Accordingly, it is necessary to urge them, but with this caution: we must not force any one to belief or to the Sacrament, nor make any law prescribing time or place; but we ought to preach so that they come without our laws and, as it were, force us, their pastors, to give them the Sacrament. This we may do by saying to them, "Whoever does not seek or desire the Sacrament, or demand it, at least once or four times a year, it is to be feared that he despises the Sacrament and is no Christian, just as he is no Christian who does not believe in or listen to the Gospel; for Christ did not say, 'Omit or despise this,' but *'This do as oft as ye drink it,'* etc." He will surely have it done, and on no account neglected or despised. *"This do,"* He says.

But if there be any one who does not greatly prize the Sacrament, that is a sign that he has no sin, no flesh, no devil, no world, no death, no danger, no hell; that is, he believes in none, though he is head over heels therein and doubly the devil's. On the other hand, he needs no mercy, life, paradise, kingdom of heaven, Christ, God, or anything that is good. For if he believed that he had so much evil and needed so much good, he would not neglect the Sacrament, in which so much help is given against evil, and so much good is bestowed. We should not then need to drive him to the Sacrament by any law, but he would come running and hurrying thither of his own accord, constrain himself, and urge you, that you should give him the Sacrament.

So thou must not establish any law herein like the Pope. Only dwell on the good and harm, necessity and blessing, the danger and salvation, in the Sacrament, and then they will come of their own accord, without your constraining them. But if they do not come, let them go their ways, and tell them they are the devil's, since they neither regard nor feel their own great need and God's gracious help. But if thou do not dwell on this, or if thou make a law and poison of it, then it is thy fault that they despise the Sacrament. How can they be otherwise than indifferent if thou sleep or keep silence? Therefore see to it, pastor and preacher! Our office has now become a different thing from what it was under the Pope: it has now become a real and saving office. Therefore it is more troublesome and full of labour, and is more encompassed by danger and temptation, and, moreover, brings little reward and thanks in this world. But Christ Himself will be our reward if we work faithfully. And so may the Father of all mercy help us, to whom be praise and thanks everlasting, through Christ our Lord. Amen.

THE SHORT CATECHISM

Translated by Henry Wace and C. A. Buchheim [1]

I. THE TEN COMMANDMENTS

How the master of the house should teach them simply to his household.

The First Commandment

Thou shalt have none other gods but me.
What does that mean?
Answer. We are to fear, love, and trust God above all things.

The Second Commandment

Thou shalt not take the name of the Lord thy God in vain.

---

[1] WACE, HENRY, and C. A. BUCHHEIM, "Luther's Primary Works," pp. 6–9.

What does that mean?

Answer. We are to fear and love God, so that we use not His name in cursing, swearing, witchcraft, lying, or deceiving, but in all our necessities call upon it, with prayer, praise, and thanks.

The Third Commandment

Remember that thou keep holy the Sabbath day.

What does that mean?

Answer. We are to fear and love God, that we despise not preaching nor His word, but keep that word holy, and gladly hear it and learn it. . . .

.   .   .   .

II. THE CREED

How the master of the house is to explain it as simply as possible to his household.

The First Article: of the Creation

I believe in God the Father Almighty, Maker of heaven and earth.

What does that mean?

Answer. I believe that God has created me and all other creatures, and has given me, and preserves for me, body and soul, eyes, ears, and all my limbs, my reason and all my senses; and that daily He bestows on me clothes and shoes, meat and drink, house and home, wife and child, fields and cattle, and all my goods, and supplies in abundance all needs and necessities of my body and life, and protects me from all perils, and guards and defends me from all evil. And this He does out of pure fatherly and Divine goodness and mercy, without any merit or worthiness in me; for all which I am bound to thank Him and praise Him, and, moreover, to serve and obey Him. This is a faithful saying.

Of the Holie Catechism

Translated by Capt. Henrie Bell [1]

That the Catechism must remain

The Catechism must remain, (said Luther) and must keep the Government in the Church, it must bee and remain Lord and Ruler. That is, the Ten Commandements, The Creed, The Lord's Praier, the Sacraments, etc. And although there bee many that set themselvs against the same, yet it shall remain and stand fast, and shall also keep the preheminence and upper hand through Him, of whom it is written, *Thou art a Priest for ever;* For Hee will bee Priest, and will also have Priests maugre [2] the Divel in Hell, and in despight of all his instruments on earth. Hee hath already fought two battels, the one with *T. M.* the other with *L. X*mo.[3] both which by their disciples are still proclaimed for saints.

[1] BELL, CAPT. HENRIE, "Dr. Martin Luther's Divine Discourses at His Table," etc., pp. 175–176.

[2] In spite of.

[3] Probably Thomas More, author of "Utopia," and Leo X; Luther was bitterly opposed to both.

That the Catechism is necessarie in the Church, specially for the Children

The common and publique Sermons (said Luther) do very little edifie the Children, who observ and learn but little thereby: but more needful it is, that they bee taught and well instructed with diligence in Schools, and at home in Houses that they bee orderly heard and examined what they have learned, that cours profiteth much. Indeed the same is very wearisom and a great trouble, but it is very necessarie. The Papists flie from such labor and pains, they trouble themselvs rather with keeping records of their rents and customs, insomuch as among them the little heap of Christians by that means is neglected and forsaken.

That the Catechism is the best and most necessarie Doctrine in the Church

My advice is, (said Luther) that wee dispute not much of Mysteries and hidden things, but rather cleav simply to God's Word, specially the Catechism; for therein wee have a very exact, a right and direct brief waie to the whole Christian Religion, and briefly therein are comprehended the chief Heads and Articles. For God Himself gave the Ten Commandements, Christ Himself penned and taught the Lord's Praier, the holie Ghost most compendiously did fasten and comprehend the Articles of Faith. These three pieces are set down and described so excellently, so comfortably and briefly, that they never could have been better performed. But they are by us slighted and contemned as things of small value, by reason the little Children daily saie and rehears the same.

The Catechism (said Luther) is the most compleat and best Doctrine, therefore it should continually bee preached, and not intermitted; all other common and publique preaching should bee grounded and built thereupon. I could wish, that wee preached it daily, and plainly read it out of the Book. But our Preachers and Hearers have it at their fingers ends, they have already swallowed it all up, they are ashamed of this slight and simple Doctrine, (as they hold it) and will bee held in higher esteem and regard, and will preach of deeper Learning. Our Parishioners saie, What, our Preachers fiddle alwaies one Lesson, they preach nothing but the Catechism, The Ten Commandements, The Creed, Of the Lord's Praier, Of Baptism and the Lord's Supper. All these wee know well enough alreadie, etc. Insomuch that our Preachers now imploie themselvs in and about higher things, they preach such points wherein the Hearers take delight, and thereby they leav and forsake the strong Foundation on which wee all ought to build.

Of the Contents and Summ of the Catechism

The Catechism (said Luther) is the right Bible of the Laitie; wherein is conteined the whole Summ of Christian Doctrine, necessarie to bee known of every Christian to Salvation . . .

Recommends the Establishment of Universities and Primary Schools

Translated by Preserved Smith and Charles M. Jacobs [1]

Luther to the Margrave George of Brandenburg.

Wittenberg, July 18, 1529.

. . . It would be good if in your Grace's principality your Grace would establish one or two universities, where not only the Holy Scriptures, but law and all the sciences would be taught. From these schools learned men could be got as preachers, pastors, secretaries, councilors, etc., for the whole principality. To this purpose the income of the monasteries and foundations could be applied so that scholars could be maintained in the schools at proper salaries, viz., two theologians, two jurists, one professor of medicine, one mathematician, and for logic, rhetoric, etc., four or five men.

For, if studying is to be good you must have not empty cloisters and deserted monasteries and endowed churches, but a city, in which many people come together and practice on one another and stir each other up and drive each other on. Solitary studies do not accomplish this, but common studies do, for where many are together one gives another incentive and example.

[1] "Luther's Correspondence and Other Contemporary Letters," translated and edited by Preserved Smith, Ph.D., and Charles M. Jacobs, D.D., pp. 486–488.

In the third place, it is well that in all towns and villages good primary schools should be established out of which could be picked and chosen those who were fit for the universities, out of which the men can then be taken who are to serve your land and people. If the towns or their citizens cannot do this, then it would be well to establish new stipends for the support of a few bright fellows in the deserted monasteries, so that every town might have one or two students. In the course of time, when the common people see that their sons can become pastors and preachers, and get other offices, many of those who now think that a scholar cannot get a living will again keep their sons in school.

If some of the scholars who are trained in these schools take service and hold office in the dominions of other lords, it must be remembered that this does no harm, for, beyond a doubt, these men will promote the founding and endowment of schools in the lands of other princes and peoples, etc.

This is the advice, that, in my little wisdom, I have desired to give your Grace. God grant your Grace His Holy Spirit to improve on all this, and in all things perfectly to do His will. Amen.

Your Grace's obedient servant,

MARTIN LUTHER.

EARLY PROTESTANT EDUCATORS

Sermon on the Duty of Sending Children to School

Translated by F. V. N. Painter [1]

This lengthy discourse ranks along with the "Letter
to the Mayors and Councilmen" six years earlier. During the interval the survey had taken place and some
efforts were made toward the establishing of schools.
In former times education had had very close relation
to the question of a livelihood for the child. The destruction of the monasteries, the changes in the cathedrals and the schools, and the suppression of the priesthood had put an end to a large number of stipends,
pensions, and other means of support. Parents no
longer felt that an education insured livings for their
children, and they consequently lost interest in sending
them to school. Luther had a deep conviction in regard
to the importance of family discipline and the necessity
of sending children to school to prepare for the vocations of the new social order. The knight, the monk,
the priest, the clerk were all passing away; new vocations were arising; pastors, teachers, lawyers, physicians, jurists, and civil servants were required to serve
the princes and the states. To prepare a sufficient number of learned men for such positions Luther urged the

[1] Painter, F. V. N., "Luther on Education," pp. 210–271.
Translation from the Leipzig edition. Original also found in
Weimar edition, "D. Martin Luthers Werke," Vol. XXX. Re-
printed by permission of Concordia Publishing House, St.
Louis, Mo.

people to send their sons to schools. This discourse was sent to the pastors to be delivered by them to the people.

DEDICATORY LETTER

To the Honorable Lazarus Spengler, Counselor of the City of Nuremberg.

MY DEAR SIR AND FRIEND: Grace and peace in Christ, our dear Lord and faithful Saviour, Amen.

I have prepared a sermon to the preachers, who are scattered here and there, on the duty of admonishing their people to send their children to school; and it has so grown on my hands as to become in fact a book, though I have been obliged to restrain myself lest it become too large, so rich and fruitful is the subject. Desiring that it might accomplish much good, I have sent it forth under your name, with no other purpose than that it might thereby attract more attention, and be read, if it is worthy, among your citizens. For, although I can well believe that your preachers are active enough, and that they, as highly favored of God, recognize and further this interest, so that—thanks be to God—they do not need my admonition and instruction; yet it does no harm that many agree in this matter, and thus present a stronger front to the devil.

For in such a great city and among so many citizens, the devil will certainly try his art and tempt some to despise the Word of God; and in particular, since commerce and

101

trade will present many occasions for it, he will seek to turn the children from education to the service of Mammon. No doubt this is now occupying his thoughts; for if he should succeed in having the Word and schools neglected in Nuremberg, he would have accomplished a great task, since he would have set an example that would have much weight in all Germany, and deal a heavy blow to education in other cities. For Nuremberg truly shines in Germany as a sun among the moon and stars, and powerfully influences the life of other communities.

But thanks and praises be to God, who long ago anticipated the devil's thoughts and caused your honorable Council to establish such an excellent school that without boasting I may say that no other university, not even that of Paris, has been better provided with teachers, as all must testify who are acquainted with such institutions. For my part I am acquainted with them only too well! But that institution is an ornament to your city, and is widely celebrated, like the wise Council who, in its establishment, showed a Christian regard for their subjects, and provided, not only for their eternal weal, but also for their temporal needs and honor. Which work God will certainly continue to strengthen more and more with His blessing and grace, though the devil struggle against it for a time; for he can not see with pleasure that such a tabernacle be built to our God in this sun among cities, and he collects clouds, mists, and dust, so that its splendor may be obscured and darkened. And how could he do otherwise?

Accordingly I hope that the citizens will recognize the

fidelity and love of such Councillors, and help earnestly to strengthen the work by keeping their children at school, since they see that without cost to themselves their children have been richly and assiduously provided for. Especially should the preachers urge it; for where they do not do so, the ordinary man is tempted and deceived by Satan, so that he easily loses sight of his duty, and fails to realize, by reason of his manifold employments, the benefits and injury at stake. Therefore we should exercise patience, when the people are not obdurate and wicked. For I know that Nuremberg has many citizens who, God be thanked, gladly do their duty when they recognize or are taught it—a glory they have not only with me, but also throughout Germany.

But it will not fail that some worshiper of Mammon will withdraw his son from school and say that "a knowledge of arithmetic and reading is enough, since we now have German books, etc.," and thus set a bad example before pious citizens, who follow him to their injury, in the opinion that he has done well. In this matter preachers can be of service. For a congregation, and especially a large city must have not only merchants, but also people who know more than arithmetic and reading in German books. German books are made especially for the common man to read at home. But for preaching, governing, and directing, both in the spiritual and the secular sphere, all the sciences and languages of the world are insufficient, let alone the German, particularly at this time when we have to speak with more people than neighbor Jack. But these devotees of Mammon do not think of government, nor consider that without preaching and ruling they would not be able to serve their idol for an hour.

I must believe that among so many people there are a few who do not care about the honor or shame of the excellent city of Nuremberg, so they get their penny. But we should pay no attention to such hurtful Mammon worshipers, but consider that, as it is a high honor for such a city to have an honorable Council providing faithfully for schools, so it would be a great shame for the citizens to despise the fidelity of their rulers, and thus make themselves participators in the bad example and scandal that would be set before other cities, which might afterwards say, "That is the way they do at Nuremberg: why should we do better?"

But if you idolaters will not consider what is godly and honorable, and will think only of Mammon, God will find others to do His work. For I have known cities, thanks be to God, in which, when the Council showed itself indifferent to schools, the pious citizens took the matter in hand and compelled the Council to establish schools and provide ministers. In like manner at Nuremberg, if God wills, the shame of your evil example will not be permitted to influence the people to despise the schools, which an honorable Council, with great fidelity and expense, has established.

But whither, my dear friend, am I running with my letter? It is one of those things which a person can say a great deal about; but I wish herewith, in your name, to speak to all your citizens, and I beg you not to think evil of me; but, as you have hitherto done, to help forward the cause. God knows I mean well. May Christ our Lord strengthen and preserve you against that day, when if God will, we shall with joy behold each other in another form. For He who has hitherto enabled you to do so much in His work and Word, will continue and finish it, to whom be praise and thanksgiving forever. Amen.

Your obedient,

MARTIN LUTHER.

Wittenberg, 1530.

To all Pastors and Preachers, my dear Friends, who love Christ in sincerity.

Martin Luther.

Grace and peace in Christ Jesus our Lord.

MY VERY DEAR SIRS AND FRIENDS: You see plainly how Satan is now attacking us on all sides, both with power and cunning, and brings about every misery, that he may destroy the holy Gospel and the kingdom of God, or, if he can not destroy it, that he may at least hinder it in every way, and prevent its progress and success. Among his various crafty devices, one of the greatest, if not the greatest, is to delude the common people into withholding their children from school and instruction, while he suggests to them such hurtful thoughts as these: "Since there is no hope for the cloisters and priesthood as formerly, we do not need learned men and study, but must consider how we may obtain food and wealth."

That is a master-piece of Satanic art; since he sees that he can not have his way in our times, he thinks to accomplish his purpose with our descendants, whom before our eyes he seeks to withhold from learning and knowledge. And thus, when we are dead, he will have a naked and defenseless people before him, with whom he can do as he pleases. For if the Scriptures and learning perish, what will remain in Germany, but a lawless horde of Tartars or Turks, yea, a multitude of wild beasts? Such results he does not allow to appear at present, and powerfully blinds the people, that when the evil does come, and they are obliged to learn it from experience, he may laugh at their misery and lamentation, which they can no longer do any thing to help. They will then be forced to say. "We have waited too long," and would give a hundred florins for half a scholar, while now they would not give five florins for a thorough one.

And because they are not willing now to support and keep pious, honorable, and skillful school-masters and teachers who at small expense and with great industry and pains would educate their children in the fear of God, in science, doctrine, and honor, it would almost serve them right to have again, as in former times, a set of ignorant and unprincipled pedagogues who at great cost would teach their children nothing but to be blockheads, and who besides would dishonor their wives, daughters, and maid-servants. Such will be the reward of their great, shameful ingratitude, into which the devil so cunningly leads them.

Since now as pastors we are to watch against these and other wicked devices, we must not sleep, but advise, urge, and admonish, with all might, industry, and care, that the common people may not allow themselves to be deceived and led astray by the devil. Therefore let every one take heed to himself and to his office that he may not sleep and thus let the devil become god and lord; for if we are silent and sleep, so that the youth are neglected and our descendants become Tartars or wild beasts, we will have to bear the responsibility and render a heavy account.

Although I know that many of you, without my admonition, attend to this matter faithfully (in reference to which I formerly addressed a special treatise to the Mayors and Aldermen of the German cities), yet, if some perchance forget it, or wish to follow my example in laboring at it more diligently, I send you this sermon, which I have more than once delivered to our people here, that you may see that I strive earnestly with you, and that we thus everywhere do our duty and in our office are justified before God. Much depends truly upon us, since we see that some who are even called ministers, go about the matter as if they wished to let all schools, discipline, and doctrine perish, or even to help to destroy them, since they cannot, as hitherto, lead the wanton life to which Satan impels them. God help us, Amen.

The Sermon

Inasmuch as I see, dear friends, that the common people are placing themselves in opposition to the schools, and that they wish to bring up their children without other instruction than that pertaining to their bodily wants; and inasmuch also as they do not consider what a fearful and un-christian course they are thus pursuing, and what a great and murderous injury they are inflicting, in the service of Satan, upon society, I have undertaken to address you this admonition, in the hope that perchance there are some who yet in some measure at least believe that there is a God in heaven, and a hell ready for the wicked (for all the world acts just as if there were neither a God in heaven nor devils in hell), and in the hope also that there are some who will heed the admonition after contemplating the advantages and disadvantages of education.

We will first consider the subject in its spiritual or eternal aspects, and afterward in its temporal or secular relations. I trust that believers and all who wish to be called Christians understand that the ministerial office was instituted of God, not with gold and silver, but with the precious blood and bitter death of his only Son, our Lord Jesus Christ. For from His wounds, (as is shown in the epistles) truly flow the sacraments, and His blood has dearly purchased for mankind the blessing of the ministerial office, the function of which is to preach, baptize, loose, bind, dispense the sacraments, comfort, warn, admonish with God's Word, and do whatever else pertains to the care of souls. Such an office not only promotes temporal life and every secular condition, but it also gives eternal life, releases from death and sin, which is its peculiar and distinguished work; and indeed the world stands and abides only on account of this office, without which it would long since have perished.

But I do not mean the clerical office, with its celibate manner of life, as seen in the cloisters and cathedrals; for it has there degenerated from its original excellent purpose, and become a device for obtaining money and contributions from the people; it has nothing clerical about it but celibacy, which is not necessary, and it consists alone in external, worldly display; for the Word of God and the work of preaching are totally disregarded. Where the Scriptures are neglected, there the clergy must be worthless.

But I mean the clerical office which pays attention to preaching and the ministration of the Word and Sacraments; which imparts the Holy Spirit and salvation—blessings not to be obtained by means of music and display; which includes the duties of pastor, teacher, preacher, reader, chaplain, sexton, and schoolmaster; and which is highly praised and extolled in the Scriptures. St. Paul speaks of ministers as the stewards and servants of God, bishops, prophets, and also ambassadors of God to reconcile the world to God (2 Cor. v. 20). Joel calls them the Lord's messengers; and Malachi says, "The priest's lips should keep knowledge; for he is the messenger of the Lord of hosts" (Mal. ii. 7); as Christ also says, Matt. xi. 10, when he calls John the Baptist a messenger, and also throughout the book of Revelation.

The ancients were very loth to assume this office on account of its great worth and responsibility, and they had to be urged and forced to do so; but afterwards, and up to the present time, there have been many who have praised the office on account of the mass more than on account of preaching, which praise has increased to such a point that the priests are exalted above Mary and the angels, because the angels and Mary cannot celebrate mass. A new priest and a first mass have been held of great importance, and blessed has been the mother that has borne a priest; but the Word of God and the work of preaching, which is the highest function of the clerical office, have been disregarded. And in a word, a man who could celebrate mass, has been called a priest, although he has not been able to preach at all, and has been only an unlearned ass; and such for the most part is the clerical office to-day.

If it is certain and true that God has instituted the office of the ministry with His own blood and death, we may be sure that He desires to have it highly honored, and continued till the day of judgment. For the Gospel and Christianity must abide till that day, as Christ says, Matt. xxviii. 20: "Lo, I am with you alway, even unto the end." But through whom is it to be continued? Oxen and horses, dogs and swine, will not do it, nor wood and stone; it must be done by men: for this office has not been committed to oxen and horses, but to men. But where shall we find persons for this work, except among those who have children? If you refuse to bring up your child for it, and others do the same, so that no fathers and mothers give their children to our God, how can the ministerial office be filled? The present incumbents can not live forever, but are dying daily; and if there are none to take their places, what will God say? Do you suppose it will be pleasing to Him that an office, divinely instituted for His honor and glory, and our salvation, is shamefully despised and with base ingratitude allowed to perish?

He has given the children and the means of their support, not that you might simply have pleasure in them and bring them up for worldly display. You are earnestly commanded to bring them up for the service of God; and otherwise you will perish with your children, as the First Commandment says: "I the Lord thy God am a jealous God, visiting the iniquity of the fathers upon the children unto the third and fourth generation of them that hate me." [1]

But how will you bring them up to the service of God when preaching and ministerial office have passed away? And the fault is yours, since you might have helped to preserve them, if you had instructed your child. For when you can teach your child, and it is capable and desirous of learning, and you do not aid but hinder it, (mark my words well!) you are responsible for the injury that comes to the world through the decline of the ministry and the neglect of God and His word. Such is your responsibility if you let the ministry decline; and if you do not feel enough interest to give your child, you would act the same if all the children in the world were yours,—so that as far as you are concerned the service of God would perish.

And it does no good to say: "My neighbor keeps his son at school, I dare not do it," and so forth. For your neighbor can say the same thing, and so on with all neighbors; and

[1] Deut. v. 9.

III

where then will God find people for the ministerial office? You have children, and can give them, but will not do it; thus, so far as you are concerned, the ministry falls to the ground. And because you with gross ingratitude let the sacred office, so dearly purchased, languish and die, you will be accursed, and in your own person, or in your children, you will suffer shame and sorrow, or otherwise be so tormented, that you will be damned with them, not only here on earth, but eternally in hell. This will not fail to come upon you, in order that you may learn that your children are not so entirely your own, that you can withhold them from God; He will have justice, and they are more His than yours.

PART FIRST

THE SPIRITUAL BENEFIT OR INJURY ARISING FROM THE SUPPORT OR NEGLECT OF SCHOOLS

And that you may not think that I speak too harshly, I will lay before you in part (for who can tell all?) the benefit or the injury that you are doing, so that, in case you find yourself guilty, and do not amend your ways, you will be obliged to say yourselves, that you verily belong to the devil and deserve to be condemned to hell; or so that, on the other hand, you may heartily rejoice and be glad if you find yourself chosen of God, to educate with your means and labor a son, who will become a pious Christian pastor, preacher, or school-master, and thus to bring up for God an especial servant—yea, as was said above, a messenger of God, a pious bishop, a saviour of many people, a king and prince in the kingdom of Christ, a teacher among God's people, a light of the world. And who will or can relate all the honor and excellence that a good and faithful pastor has before God? There is no more precious treasure, no nobler thing on earth, than a pious, faithful pastor or preacher.

For consider that whatever of good is connected with the office of preaching and the care of souls, will be accomplished by your son, if he is faithful in his ministry, so that through him many souls will be daily taught, converted, baptized, brought to Christ, made blessed, redeemed from sin, death, hell, and the devil, and come to perfect righteousness and eternal life in heaven. Daniel well says: "They that teach others shall shine as the brightness of the firmament; and they that turn many to righteousness, as the stars forever and ever" (Dan. xii. 3). For since God's Word and office, where they are rightly employed, must always accomplish great things, and indeed work miracles, your son will be constantly doing wonderful things for God, such as to raise the dead, cast out devils, make the blind to see, the deaf to hear, the lepers to be clean, the dumb to speak, and the lame to walk. If this is not done in the body, it is done in the soul, which is indeed a greater work, as Christ says, John xiv. 12: "He that believeth on me, the works that I do shall he do also; and greater works than these shall he do." If a simple Christian can do such things in the case of individuals, how much more can a public preacher accomplish, who deals with whole congregations? Not that he does it himself, but his office, which has been instituted of God for that purpose, and the Word of God, which he teaches; for he is but an instrument in the hands of God.

If he does such great works and miracles spiritually, it follows that he does them also physically, or at least is a beginner and cause of them. For whence comes it that Christians will rise from the dead on the day of judgment? —that all the deaf, blind, lame, and all other sufferers will throw off their bodily ailments, and that their bodies will not simply become beautiful and sound, but, as Christ says, shine bright and glorious as the sun? Does it not come from the fact that here on earth, through the Word of God, they have been converted, baptized, and united to Christ? As Paul says, Rom. viii. 11: "He that raised up Christ from the dead shall also quicken your mortal bodies by His Spirit that dwelleth in you." Who helps men to such faith, and the beginning of the bodily resurrection, without the office of preaching and the Word of God, which are committed to your son? Is that not an immeasurably grander and more splendid work and miracle, than if He raised the dead here in the world, and restored the blind, deaf, dumb, and leprous to a perishable existence?

If you were certain that your son would perform one of these works on a single individual, so that he would make a blind man to see, raise a man from the dead, rescue a soul from the devil, or save a human being from hell, would you not properly, with all joy, use your means to educate him for such an office and work? And would you not leap for joy that with your money you had accomplished so great a thing for God? For what are all endowments and cloisters, as they now exist with their own works, in comparison with such a pastor, preacher, or school-master? although in former times they were established by pious kings and lords for this precious end, that they might be agencies for bringing up such pastors and preachers; but now alas! through the influence of the devil, they have sunk into degradation, so that they have become, to the injury and destruction of Christianity, the suburbs of hell.

Behold, thy son performs not only one such work, but many, and that every day; and what is best of all, he does them in the sight of God, who holds them dear, as has been shown, though men do not recognize and esteem them; yea, if the world regard him as a heretic, seducer, deceiver, so much the better: it is a good sign that he is an upright man, and like the Lord Jesus Christ. For Christ himself was held a deceiver, rebel, and criminal, and was judged and crucified with murderers. Were I a preacher, what would it concern me that the world called me a devil, if I knew that God called me an angel? Let the world call me a seducer as long as it pleases—if God but call me his faithful servant and steward, the angels call me their companion, the saints call me their brother, the believing call me their father, distressed souls call me their saviour, the ignorant call me their light, and God approves of it all, what harm can the world and the devil do me with their calumny and abuse?

We have been speaking of the works and miracles which your son does in relation to souls, in saving them from sin, death, and the devil. But in relation to the world also he does great and mighty works, in that he informs and instructs all classes how they are to discharge their various duties in a manner acceptable to God. He comforts the sorrowing, gives counsel, settles difficulties, calms disturbed consciences, helps to maintain peace, to appease, to reconcile, and similar duties without number; for a preacher confirms, strengthens, and supports all authority, all temporal peace, governs the seditious, teaches obedience, morality, discipline, and honor, and gives instruction in the duties pertaining to fathers, mothers, children, servants, and in a word to all other secular relations of life. These are, it is true, the least of a pastor's services; yet they are so excellent and noble that the wisest of the heathen philosophers did not recognize or understand, much less practice them; and no jurist, no university, no cloister, knows of such works, nor are they taught in either ecclesiastical or civil law. For there is no one who recognizes such secular offices as the great gifts or gracious arrangement of God; it is the Word of God and the ministerial offices alone that highly praise and honor them.

Therefore, if we wish to speak the truth, we must say that temporal peace—the greatest good on earth, in which all other temporal blessings are comprehended—is really a fruit of the ministerial office. For where it perishes, there are found war, hatred, and the shedding of blood; and where it is not properly exercised, we find, if not actual war, at least a constant unrest, a desire for war and bloodshed. We see this exemplified in the case of the Papists, who can do nothing but shout fire and blood, and who murder innocent pastors on account of marriage, though the Pope himself and their own ecclesiastical law only sanction as the highest punishment for such an offense expulsion from the priestly office, according the offenders life, and property, and Christian integrity; and so far from condemning them to hell, they do not even hold them as heretics, as all the jurists and the world at large must testify, and as the imperial Diet at Nuremberg decreed. But the blind bloodhounds who have turned the clerical office into a lie, can not desist from murder, as their god the devil also does, who from the beginning has been a murderer and liar. (John viii. 44.)

An upright pastor, then, serves mankind in body and soul, in estate and honor. But above that, consider how he serves God, and what splendid sacrifices and services he renders: for through his office and Word, the kingdom of God is maintained in the world, the honor, the name, the glory of God, a right faith and apprehension of Christ, the fruit of the suffering, and blood, and death of Christ, the gifts, works and power of the Holy Spirit, the proper use of Baptism and the Lord's supper, the pure doctrine of the Gospel, the proper manner of chastening and crucifying the flesh, and similar blessings. Who can sufficiently extol a single one of them? And how much remains to be said! The faithful pastor fights against the devil, worldly wisdom, spiritual blindness; he gains victories over them, strikes down error, suppresses heresies. For he must strive and battle against the gates of hell, overcome the devil, which he also does, not by his own might, but through his office and word. These are all inexpressible works and miracles of the ministerial office. In a word, if we praise God himself, we must also praise the Word and preaching; for it is the office and Word of God.

If you were a king, you should yet esteem yourself unworthy to consecrate your son, with all your property, to such an office and work. Is not the labor or the penny that you bestow on such a son, too highly honored, too richly blessed, too costly invested, and in the eyes of God is it not better than any kingdom or empire? A man ought to carry such a penny to the ends of the earth, if he knew that it would be so splendidly invested. And behold, you have in your own house and in your own bosom the means of this priceless investment. Shame, and again I say shame upon our blind and base ingratitude, that we do not see what a beautiful and excellent service we render to God, yea, what great personages we may become in His sight, with little effort and expense.

The Papists abuse us Lutherans for not teaching good works. They are fine fellows to talk about good works! Are not the things just mentioned good works? What are all the works of the priests and monks in comparison with such miracles? Their talk is like the chattering of jackdaws, only not so good; for the jackdaws chatter from love and pleasure, but the Papists howl from chagrin. If people have heretofore set great store by the first mass and a new priest; if father and mother with their friends have rejoiced because they had brought up a son to be an idle, lazy, useless priest of the mass or of the cupboard, who with his blasphemous sacrifice of the mass and his reprobate prayers insults God, and vexes and flays society: how much more should you rejoice, if you bring up a son for one of these callings, in which you are sure that he grandly serves God, richly aids mankind, and heroically fights the devil? Here you make a true sacrifice of your son, so that the angels are obliged to regard you with admiration.

Again, you should also know the injury you do, if you take the opposite course. For if God has given you a child suitable for such an office, and you do not bring him up for it, thinking only of his temporal wants; take up the list of good works and miracles above given, and examine it, and you will find what a hypocrite you are. For as far as lies in your power, you deprive God of a messenger, a servant, a king and prince in his kingdom, a saviour and comforter of man in body and soul, in estate and honor, a captain and knight to contend against the devil; and at the same time you make room for the devil, and advance his kingdom, by helping him to keep souls in sin, death, hell, and daily to bring many more under his power; you aid in perpetuating heresy, error, discontent, war, and hate in the world, whereby it daily becomes worse; and thus the kingdom of God, Christian faith, the fruit of the suffering and blood of Christ, the work of the Holy Spirit, the Gospel and all worship of God perish, while the service of Satan and fatal errors gain the ascendency. This condition of things would have been hindered and bettered, if you had brought up your child to the ministry.

How will it be with you, when God on your death-bed,

or in the day of judgment, thus addresses you: "I was hungry, thirsty, a guest, naked, sick, in prison, and you did not help me; for what you have not done to my people and kingdom and Gospel on earth, helping to destroy them and allowing souls to perish, you have not done to me. For you could have helped me; I had given you children and property; but you stubbornly permitted me and my kingdom and the souls of men to suffer want and to be despised, while in opposition to me you served Satan and his kingdom. He shall now be your reward; depart with him into the abyss of hell! You have not helped to build up and advance my kingdom, but to weaken and destroy it; you have helped to promote the interests and power of the devil: dwell then in the house you have built."

What do you think? Are you not in danger that the wrath of God may suddenly overtake you, who go on heedlessly, as if you were doing right in not instructing your children? And when his judgment comes, you will have to say that you are righteously condemned to hell as one of the most impious and most hurtful of men. And if you would now, in the present life, rightly consider the matter, you would be filled with terror; for no conscience is able to bear the guilt of a single one of the particulars mentioned above; how much less can it bear the burden of all when they suddenly fall upon the soul? Your heart will then cry out that your sins are more numerous than the leaves of the forest, greater than heaven and earth, and with Manasseh, king of Judah, you will exclaim: "My sins are more than the sands of the seashore, and my offense is great."

Our natural sense of right attests this truth, that who-ever can prevent an injury, and does not do it, he is guilty of the injury, since he evidently has a desire and will for it, and would do it himself, if he had cause and opportunity. Therefore such people are no better than Satan himself, because they are so hostile to God and the world, that they help to overthrow religion and social order, and faithfully serve the devil. In a word, if we can denounce Satan enough, we can denounce such people enough, who hinder the office and work ordained of God: for they are the servants of the devil.

I do not mean that every one is obliged to bring up his child to such an office, for all boys are not to become pas-tors, preachers, school-masters; and it is well to know that the children of lords and nobles are not to be thus employed, since society needs them for secular authority and social order. I speak of the common people, who would formerly have schooled their children for the sake of a benefice and an income, and who now only on account of support with-hold them from the office, although they need no heirs, and keep their children from school, notwithstanding the fact that their children are well adapted to the ministry, and could serve God without want or hindrance.

Such promising children should be instructed, especially the children of the poor; for this purpose the revenues of endowments and monasteries were provided. But also the boys that are less promising should learn at least to under-stand, read, and write Latin. For we need not only learned doctors and masters in the Scriptures, but also ordinary pastors, who may teach the Gospel and the catechism to the young and ignorant, baptize, administer the Lord's Supper, etc. If they are not capable of contending with heretics, it does not matter. For in a good building, we need both large and small timber; and in like manner we must have sextons and others to aid the minister and further the Word of God.

And if such a boy who has learned Latin afterwards works at a trade, you will have him in reserve, to labor as a pastor in case of need; and such knowledge will not interfere with his gaining a livelihood and will enable him to govern his house all the better. And especially in our times is it easy to educate such persons, who may learn the Gospel and the catechism, because not only the Holy Scriptures but also every kind of learning is now within reach, with so many books and so much reading and preaching that (God be thanked!) a man at present can learn more in three years than formerly in twenty; even women and children can now learn more of God and Christ from German books and sermons (I speak the truth) than was formerly known by the universities, priests, monks, the whole Papacy, and the entire world. But even the ordinary pastor and preacher must be acquainted with Latin, which he can no more dispense with than the learned can dispense with Greek and Hebrew, as St. Augustine says, and ecclesiastical law itself establishes.

But you say, "How if it turns out badly, so that my son becomes a heretic or a villain?" For, as people say, "education means perversion." Well, you must run that risk; but your labor is not lost. God will consider your faithful service, and will count it as if successful. You must run the risk, as in other callings to which you wish to bring up your son. How was it with Abraham, whose son Ishmael did badly; with Isaac and his son Esau; with Adam and his son Cain? Ought Abraham for that reason to have neglected his son Isaac, Isaac his son Jacob, and Adam his son Abel? Among the chosen children of Israel, how many wicked kings and people there were, who with their heresy and idolatry wrought all manner of evil and slew the prophets: would it therefore have been right for the priests to neglect the whole people, and educate no one for the service of God? How many wicked priests and Levites were in the tribe of Levi, which God himself chose for the priestly office? How many people has God on earth who abuse all his goodness? Should He therefore withhold His goodness, suffer all men to perish, and cease to do well?

You should not be anxious in regard to the support of your son in case he devotes himself to learning and the ministry, for God has not forsaken and forgotten you in this particular. He has ordained through St. Paul, 1 Cor. ix. 14, "that they which preach the Gospel should live the Gospel." And Christ himself has said, Matt. x. 10, that "the workman is worthy of his meat." In the Old Testament, in order that the ministerial office might not perish, God chose and took the whole tribe of Levi, that is to say, the twelfth part of the whole people of Israel, and gave them "the tenth in Israel for an inheritance," and in addition the first fruits, all kinds of offerings, their own cities, land, and cattle, and whatever belongs thereto. In the New Testament era, see how richly in former times emperors, kings, princes and lords, contributed to the support of this office, so that churches and monasteries now surpass kings and princes in wealth. God will not and can not forsake his faithful servants, as He has promised, Heb. xiii. 5: "I will never leave thee nor forsake thee."

Consider for yourselves how many pastorates, schools, and other offices are daily becoming vacant. That fact assures your son of a support before he needs it or has earned it. When I was a young student, I heard it said that in Saxony, if I mistake not, there were about eighteen hundred parishes. If that is true, and if with each parish two persons, a pastor and a sexton, are connected (not counting the preachers, chaplains, assistants, and teachers in the cities), it follows that about four thousand learned persons belong to such a principality, of whom one-third die in ten years. Now I would wager that there are not four thousand students in the half of Germany. I venture the assertion also that there are scarcely eight hundred pastors in Saxony;—how many must be wanting in all Germany?

I should like to know where in three years we are to get pastors, teachers, and sextons? If we remain idle, and if the princes in particular do not see to it that both preparatory schools and universities are properly maintained, there will be such a want of educated persons, that three or four cities will have to be assigned to one pastor, and ten villages to one chaplain, if perchance the ministers can be found at all.

It is sad to see how the universities of Erfurt, Leipsic, and others, as well as the preparatory schools, are deserted, so that little Wittenberg almost alone is doing its best. This same want, I imagine, will be felt also by the chapters and monasteries, who will not continue to boast as they have begun. Hence you can send your son to school with full assurance that men will be wanting rather than means; and perchance, if the world lasts and God graciously influences princes and cities to act, the property of chapters and cloisters may be applied to this purpose, for which it was originally designed. And why care so much for the body? There stands Christ and says, Matt. vi. 31, 33: "Take no thought, saying, what shall we eat? or, what shall we drink? or, wherewithal shall we be clothed? For your heavenly Father knoweth that ye have need of all these things. But seek ye first the kingdom of God and his righteousness, and all these things shall be added unto you." Whoever does not believe that, let him take anxious thought, and yet die of hunger.

Though it is true that some years ago many pastors suffered hunger and destitution, the reason is to be found in the great commotion prevailing in the world, so that people became wicked, ungrateful, and avaricious, and persecuted the Gospel! It was thus that God tried us, in order to see if we were sincere; and we are not to regard this trial otherwise than in the days of the martyrs, when pious teachers suffered great poverty and want, as St. Paul himself boasts. And Christ also predicted, Matt. ix. 15: "When the bridegroom shall be taken from them, then shall they fast." That is true, evangelical fasting.

God's Word has seldom appeared without being attended with scarcity or famine, as in the days of Abraham, Isaac, Jacob, Joseph, Elijah, Elisha; and in the early days of the Gospel, there was a "great dearth throughout all the world." (Acts xi. 28). And the blame is ascribed to be the precious Gospel and the Word of God, and not to the past sins and present obdurate ingratitude of men. Thus the Jews attributed all their misfortune to the teaching of Jeremiah (Jer. xliv. 16–19). And the Romans, when they were overthrown by the Goths, ascribed their defeat to the fact that they had become Christians, against which error St. Augustine wrote a great book, "De Civitate Dei."

But say what we will, the world is the world; as those became deceivers and perished, so shall also these become deceivers and perish, that Christ and His word may remain. He sits exalted and immovable, as it is written: "The Lord said unto my Lord, sit thou on my right hand." He can not be moved; and so long as He remains, we shall remain also. And in a word, it would be as easy for your son to secure a support from the ministry as from a trade, if property is what you are after, in order to make a great lord of your son in the eyes of the world, like the bishops and canons. But if you are thus minded, this discourse is not addressed to you.

I speak to the believing, who honor the ministerial office, and esteem it far above wealth as, next to God himself, the best treasure given to men, in order that they may know what a great service they render God, when they prefer this work with little pay to the world's riches without it.

They will not fail to recognize that the soul is more than the body, and that the body may be easily provided for, all superfluities being left behind at death. But those who seek true riches will take their treasure with them, which is far better. So much for a brief and hasty consideration of the benefit and the injury resulting from a maintenance or a neglect of the schools.

PART SECOND

THE TEMPORAL BENEFIT OR INJURY ARISING FROM THE SUPPORT OR THE NEGLECT OF SCHOOLS

The second part of this discourse will be devoted to the temporal or secular benefit and injury resulting from a support or a neglect of schools. In the first place, it is true that secular authority or station is in no way comparable to the spiritual office of the ministry, as St. Paul calls it; for it is not so dearly purchased through the blood and death of the Son of God. It can not perform such great works and miracles as the ministerial office; for all the works of secular authority belong only to this temporal and transitory existence, such as caring for body, wife, child, house, goods, and honor, and whatever pertains to the needs of the present life. As far then as eternal life surpasses temporal life, so far does the ministerial office surpass secular office; the one is the substance, the other is the shadow. For secular authority is an image, shadow, or figure of the authority of Christ; for the ministerial office, (where it exists as God

127

ordained it,) brings and imparts eternal righteousness, eternal peace, and eternal life, as St. Paul declares in the fourth chapter of 2 Corinthians. But secular government maintains temporal and transitory peace, law, and life.

But it is still a beautiful and divine ordinance, an excellent gift of God, who ordained it, and who wishes to have it maintained as indispensable to human welfare; without it men could not live together in society, but would devour one another like the irrational animals. Therefore, as it is the function and honor of the ministerial office to make saints out of sinners, to restore the dead to life, to confer blessedness upon the lost, to change the servants of the devil into children of God: so it is the function and honor of civil government to make men out of wild animals, and to restrain them from degenerating into brutes. It protects every one in body, so that he may not be injured; it protects every one in family, so that the members may not be wronged; it protects every one in house, lands, cattle, property, so that they may not be attacked, injured, or stolen.

This state of things does not exist among the lower animals, and it would not prevail among men, if it were not for civil government. If the birds and beasts could speak, and should consider the civil regulations of men, do you not suppose that they would say: "O ye men, in comparison with us ye are gods! In what security ye live and possess all things! But we are not secure against one another for an hour in life, home or food. Woe to your ingratitude, that ye do not perceive what an excellent gift the God of us all has bestowed upon you!"

Since then it is certain that civil government is a divine ordinance, an office and institution necessary for men in the present life, it is easy to see that God does not design that it should perish, but that it should continue for the protection of the righteous and the punishment of the wicked, as is clearly taught in Rom. xiii. 4 and 1 Pet. ii. 13. But who will maintain it except us men to whom God has committed it? Wild animals will not do it, wood and stone will not; but what man can maintain it? Certainly not those who rule by club-law alone, as many now think. For where club-law alone prevails, will surely be found at last a brutal condition of society, the strong tyrannizing over the weak. We have examples enough before our eyes to show us what sheer physical force, without wisdom or reason, would do.

Hence Solomon says in Prov. viii. 14, 15, that wisdom must rule, and not force, testifying of the former: "Counsel is mine and sound wisdom; I am understanding; I have strength. By me kings reign, and princes decree justice." And in Eccles. ix. 16, 18, he says: "Wisdom is better than strength. Wisdom is better than weapons of war." All history shows that mere force, without reason or wisdom, can never accomplish anything; and even tyrants and murderers, unless they wisely cloak their tyranny under the forms of law and right, can not long continue in authority, but soon disagree and perish by one another's hand. In a word, not club-law but justice, not force but wisdom and reason, must govern among the wicked as well as among the good.

Accordingly, since our government in the German states is based on the imperial law of Rome, which embodies the wisdom and reason of our government, it follows that such a government can not be maintained, unless these laws are upheld. Now who will uphold them? Club-law and force will not do it; it must be done by means of knowledge and books; men must learn and understand the law and wisdom of our empire. Although it is an excellent thing when an emperor, prince or lord is wise and judicious by nature, so that he can administer justice without external aids, as could Frederick, Duke of Saxony, and Fabian von Feilitz (not to speak of the living); yet such rulers are rare, and their example is dangerous, so that it is always better to adhere to the written law, which carries with it authority, and serves as a safeguard against arbitrary action.

Now in civil government it is the jurists and scholars who uphold this law, and thereby maintain secular authority; and just as a pious theologian or sincere preacher in the kingdom of Christ is called a messenger of God, a saviour, prophet, priest, steward and teacher (as was said above), in like manner a pious jurist or a faithful scholar in the government of the emperor might be called a prophet, priest, messenger, and saviour. On the other hand, just as a heretical minister in the kingdom of Christ is a devil, thief, murderer, blasphemer; in the same way a corrupt and unfaithful jurist in the government of the emperor is a thief, rogue, traitor, devil.

When I speak of jurists, I do not mean the doctors alone, but the whole body of civil officers—chancellors, secretaries, judges, advocates, notaries, and whatever else belongs to the civil administration, even the great crowd of advisers, as they are called, at court; for they exercise the functions of law and of jurists. And since an adviser through evil advice can easily become a traitor, it sometimes happens that under the form of friendly counsel sovereigns are basely betrayed.

You now see of what use an upright jurist can be; yea, who can fully set it forth? For whatever is God's ordinance and work, bears so much fruit that it can not be told or comprehended. First of all, such a jurist maintains and furthers with his legal knowledge (through divine institution) the whole structure of civil government—emperors, princes, lords, cities, states, people (as before stated), for all must be upheld through wisdom and justice. But who can sufficiently praise this work alone? It gives you protection of body and life against neighbors, enemies, murderers; protection also of wife, daughters, sons, house, servants, money, property, lands, and whatever you possess; for it is all comprehended, secured, and hedged about by law. How great a blessing that is, can not be told. Who can express the immeasurable benefits of peace? How much it gives and saves every year!

Such great works can your son do, and such a useful person can he become, if you direct him to the civil service and send him to school; and if you can become a sharer in this honor, and make such good use of your money, ought it not to be a great pleasure and glory to you? Think of your son as a messenger in the empire, an apostle of the emperor, a cornerstone and foundation of temporal peace on earth! Knowing, too, that God looks upon the service in this light, as indeed it deserves to be! For though we can not be justified and secure salvation by such works, it is still a joyful comfort that these works are well-pleasing to God, especially when such a man is a believer and a member of Christ's kingdom; for in that way we thank him for his benefits, and bring him the best thank-offering and the highest service.

You must indeed be an insensible and ungrateful creature, fit to be ranked among the brutes, if you see that your son may become a man to help the emperor maintain his dominions, sword, and crown—to help the prince govern his land, to counsel cities and states, to help protect for every man his body, wife, child, property, and honor—and yet will not do so much as to send him to school and prepare him for this work! Tell me, what are all the chapters and cloisters doing in comparison with this? I would not give the work of a faithful, upright jurist and secretary for the righteousness of all the monks, priests, and nuns at their best. And if such great good works do not move you, the honor and desire of God alone should move you, since you know that you thereby express your gratitude to God, and render Him a service of surpassing excellence, as has been said. It is a shameful contempt of God that you do not bring up your children to such an excellent and divinely appointed calling, and that you strengthen them only in the service of appetite and avarice, teaching them nothing but to provide for the stomach, like a hog with its nose always in filth, and do not bring them up to this worthy station and office. You must either be insensible creatures, or else you do not love your children.

But hearken further: how if God demands your child for such office? For you are under obligation to help maintain civil order if you can. Now, beyond all doubt, it can not be maintained if people do not have their children instructed; and since more wisdom is required in civil office than in the ministry, it will be necessary to set apart for it the brightest boys. For in the ministry Christ works by His Spirit; but in civil government men must be guided by reason (which is the source of human laws): for God has placed secular government and our physical state under the control of reason (Gen. ii. 19), and has not sent the Holy Spirit for that purpose. Hence the functions of civil office are more difficult than those of the ministry, since the conscience can not rule, but must act, so to speak, in the dark.

If now you have a son capable of learning; if you can send him to school, but do not do it and go your way asking nothing about temporal government, law, peace, and so on; you are, to the extent of your ability, opposing civil authority like the Turk, yea, like the devil himself. For you withhold from the empire, principality, state, city, a saviour, comforter, corner-stone, helper; and so far as you are concerned, the emperor loses both his sword and crown, the state loses protection and peace, and it is through your fault (as much as lies in you) that no man can hold in security his body, wife, child, house, property. On the contrary, you freely offer them all upon a butcher's block, and give occasion for men to degenerate into brutes, and at last to devour one another. All this you certainly do, especially if you on purpose withdraw your child from such a salutary station out of regard for his physical wants. Are you not a pretty and useful man in society! You daily enjoy the benefits of the government, and then as a return rob it of your son, dedicating him to avarice, and thus strive with all your might not to maintain government, law, and peace, but to destroy social order, though you possess and hold your body, life, property, and honor, through secular authority.

What do you think you deserve? Are you even worthy to dwell among men? What will God say, who has given you child and property that you might honor Him therewith, and consecrate your child to His service? Is it not serving God, if we help to maintain His ordinance of civil government? Now you neglect such service, as if it did not concern you, or as if you above all men were free and not bound to serve God; and you presume to do with your child what you please, even though the temporal and the spiritual kingdom of God perish; and at the same time you enjoy the protection, peace, and law of the empire, and allow the ministry and Word of God to serve you, so that God becomes your servant; and yet you abuse all these benefits to turn your son from him, and to teach him the service of Mammon.

Do you not think God will pronounce such a judgment on your worldliness that you will perish with your children and property? Rather, is not your heart affrighted at the horror of your idolatry, at your contempt of God, your ingratitude, your destruction of the civil and religious ordinances of God, yea, at the injury you do all men? Well, I have declared unto you both the benefit and injury you can do; and do which you will, God will surely repay you.

I will not here speak of the pleasure a scholar has, apart from any office, in that he can read at home all kinds of books, talk and associate with learned men, and travel and transact business in foreign lands. For this pleasure perhaps will move but few; but since you are seeking Mammon and worldly possessions, consider what great opportunities God has provided for schools and scholars; so that you need not despise learning from fear of poverty. Behold, emperors and kings must have chancellors, secretaries, counsellors, jurists and scholars; there is not a prince but must have chancellors, jurists, counsellors, scholars, and secretaries; likewise counts, lords, cities, states, castles, must have councils, secretaries, and other learned men; there is not a nobleman but must have a secretary. And to speak of ordinary scholars, where are the miners, merchants, and artisans? At the end of three years where are we to find educated men, when the want has already begun to be felt? It looks as if kings would have to become jurists, princes chancellors, counts and lords secretaries, and mayors sextons.

If we do not soon begin to do something, we shall become Tartars and Turks, and ignoramuses will again be doctors and counsellors at court. Therefore I hold that there never was a better time for study than the present, not only because learning is so accessible and cheap, but also because great wealth and honor must follow; for those who study at this time will become such valuable people that two princes and three cities will contend for one scholar. If you look about you, you will find innumerable offices that will need learned men in less than ten years, and yet but few young people are being educated for them.

There is further a divine blessing attached to this sphere of activity; for God is pleased with the many excellent and useful works that belong to the secular condition, and that constitute a divine service. But avarice in seeking its end meets with contempt (even though its works be not sinful); evil deeds destroy all peace of mind, and such a life can not be called a service of God. Now I would rather earn ten florins with a work that might properly be called a service of God, than a thousand florins with a work that could not be called a service of God, but a service of self and Mammon.

In addition to this, there is worldly honor. For chancellors, scribes, jurists, and the people through them, occupy upper seats, help, advise, and govern as said above, and in fact they here become lords on earth, though in person, birth, and station they are not so regarded. For Daniel says that he did the king's work. And it is true that a chancellor must perform imperial, kingly, princely functions and duties, a city scribe must do the work of the council and city, and that all with honor and the blessing of God, which gives happiness and salvation.

When they are not engaged in war but govern by law,

what are emperors, kings, princes, (if we speak according to their work,) but mere scribes and jurists? For they concern themselves about the law, which is a legal and clerical work. And who governs the land and people in times of peace? Is it the knights and captains? I think it is the pen of the scribe. Meanwhile, what is avarice doing with its worship of Mammon? It can not come to such honor, and defiles its devotees with its rust-covered treasures.

Thus the emperor Justinian declares that "imperial majesty ought not only to be adorned with arms, but also to be armed with laws." Observe the peculiar phraseology this emperor uses, when he calls the laws his weapons, and weapons his adornment, and changes his scribes into cuirassiers and warriors. And he spoke well; for the laws are truly the right armor and weapons with which to protect the country and people, yea, the empire and government, (as has been sufficiently shown above,) so that wisdom is better than might. And pious jurists are the real warriors that preserve the emperor and princes. How many passages, if time permitted, might be given from the poets and the historians! Solomon himself in Eccles. ix. 15 declares that a poor man by his wisdom saved a city from a powerful king.

Not that I would have soldiers, knights, and whatever else belongs to warfare, despised and repudiated; they also help (where they are obedient) to maintain peace and protect the land by force. Every thing has its honor before God, and its station and work.

I must also praise my craft, though I should be censured;

just as St. Paul constantly praised his office, so that many thought he went too far and was proud. Whoever wishes to praise and honor soldiers, can find ground enough to do so, as I have elsewhere shown in strong terms. For I do not like those jurists and scribblers who have so high an opinion of themselves that they despise or mock other callings, as the extortionate priests and other adherents of the Papacy have hitherto done.

We should duly praise all the offices and works ordained of God, and not despise one for the sake of another; for it is written, "His work is honorable and glorious" (Ps. iii. 3). And again, Ps. civ. 24: "O Lord, how manifold are thy works! in wisdom hast thou made them all." And especially should preachers constantly inculcate such thoughts upon the people, school-teachers likewise upon their pupils, and parents upon their children, that these may learn what stations and offices are ordained of God. When they come to understand this, they should not despise, mock, or speak evil of them, but honor and esteem them. That is pleasing to God, and contributes to peace and unity; for God is a great Lord, and has many servants.

On the contrary, we find some conceited soldiers that fancy the name scribe is not worthy to be mentioned or heard by them. Well, pay no attention to it, but consider that these poor fellows must have some kind of pastime and pleasure. Let them make the most out of this; but you still remain a scribe in the eyes of God and the world. If they come together for any length of time, you see that they bestow the highest honor upon the quill, placing a feather on

hat or helmet, as if they confessed by that act that the pen
is the most excellent thing in the world, without which they
would not be equipped for combat, nor for parade in times
of peace, much less assemble in security; for they must also
profit by the peace which the emperor's preachers and teachers (the jurists) maintain. Therefore, as you see, they give
the place of honor to the instrument of our craft (and properly), since they gird the sword about the loins; there it
hangs handsomely for their purpose: on the head it would
not be becoming—there the feather must wave. If they have
sinned against you, they have thus made atonement and
should be forgiven.

The work of the scholar, as I have shown, is not appreciated by many ignoramuses; for they do not know that it is a
divine office and function, nor consider how necessary and
useful it is to the world. But let them go, and look about you
for wise and pious noblemen, as Duke George of Werdheim,
Hans von Schwartzenberg, George von Fronsberg, and
others of blessed memory, (I shall not speak of the living,)
and comfort yourself in them. Consider that God, for the
sake of one man, Lot, honored the whole city of Zoar; for
the sake of Naaman, the whole land of Syria; and for the
sake of Joseph, the whole kingdom of Egypt; and why
should not you, for the sake of many worthy men, honor all
the nobility? Think rather of the good than of the bad. Do
not condemn the tree, because perchance some of its fruit
falls untimely or becomes a prey to worms.

Thus do the children of God. For God spares the whole
human race for the sake of one man, who is called Jesus

Christ. If he were to look on mankind alone, there could be nothing but anger. Yet the ministry and the civil authorities are necessarily required to pay attention to evil, for they should punish the wicked; some by reproof, and some by the sword. But we should learn to distinguish between what is God's work and what is man's wickedness. In all divine offices and stations there are many wicked men; but the office still remains good, however much men may abuse it. We find, for example, many bad women, dishonest servants, and injurious officers and counsellors; and yet all these relations and conditions are the work and ordinance of God. The sun remains good, though the whole world abuse its light, some to rob, some to murder, and some to work other evils. Who could do evil if the sun did not give light, if the earth did not bring forth fruit, if the air did not remain pure, and if God did not thus exercise a constant care? It is written, "The creature was made subject to vanity, not willingly," Rom. viii. 20.

There are some who think that the office of scribe is an easy, insignificant office, but that to ride in armor and suffer heat, frost, dust, thirst, and other discomforts, is work. Verily that is an old story—no one knows where the shoe pinches another; every one feels only his own discomfort, and looks only at the comforts of another. It is true that it would be hard for me to ride in armor; but I should like to see the knight who could sit still the whole day and look in a book, though he were not required to read, think, or do any thing. Ask a chancery-clerk, preacher, orator, about the labor of writing and speaking; ask a school-master about the labor of teaching boys. The pen is a light instrument, it is true, and among all the trades there is no tool more easily procured than the pen; for it needs only a goose-quill, which can be found anywhere. But the best part of the body, as the head, and the noblest member, as the tongue, and the highest function, as speech, must here bear the brunt, and do most of the work, while in other occupations it is the hands, feet, back that labor, and the workman can at the same time sing and joke, which a writer must forego. Three fingers do it, (as is said of writers,) but the whole body and soul work at the same time.

When the ignoramuses about the illustrious emperor Maximilian complained that he employed so many scribes for embassies and other similar duties, he is said to have replied: "What shall I do? You can not be employed, so I must take scribes." And further: "I can make knights, but not doctors." I have heard also of a wise nobleman who said: "I shall let my son study; there is no great art in straddling a horse and becoming a knight,—a thing that is soon learned." And that is all well said.

I do not say this to depreciate the knightly order or any other, but to rebuke the ignorant fellows who despise all learning and culture, and praise nothing but wearing armor and straddling a horse, though they are seldom obliged to do it, and hence, the whole year through, have comfort, pleasure, honor, and money. It is indeed true that learning is light to carry, and that armor is heavy to carry; but on the other hand, to wear armor is easily learned, but an education is neither quickly acquired nor easily employed.

But to make an end of this matter, God is a wonderful sovereign, and it is his plan of work to make lords out of beggars, as he made the heaven and earth out of nothing; and in this no man will hinder Him, who is praised in all the world, as the 112th Psalm says: "Who is like unto the Lord our God, who dwelleth on high, who humbleth Himself to behold the things that are in heaven and in the earth? He raiseth up the poor out of the dust, and lifteth the needy out of the dunghill; that He may set him with princes, even with the princes of His people." Look at all the courts of kings and princes, and in cities and pastorates, and do you not see this Psalm fulfilled by many striking examples? You will there find jurists, doctors, counselors, scribes, preachers, who struggled with poverty in acquiring an education, and who have risen by means of the pen to the position of lords, as this Psalm says, and like princes they help to govern the land and people. God does not wish that those who are born kings, princes, lords, and nobles should alone rule, but He desires also to have His beggars share in the government; otherwise, they would think that noble birth alone made lords and rulers, and that God had nothing to do with it.

It is true, as is sometimes said, that the Pope was once a student; therefore do not despise the boys who beg from door to door "a little bread for the love of God,"[1] and when the groups of poor pupils sing before your house, remember that you hear, as this Psalm says, great princes and lords. I have myself been such a beggar pupil, and have eaten bread

[1] *Panem propter Deum.*

142

before houses, especially in the dear town of Eisenach,
though afterwards my beloved father supported me at the
University of Erfurt with all love and self-sacrifice, and by
the sweat of his face helped me to the position I now occupy;
but still I was for a time a poverty student, and according
to this Psalm I have risen by the pen to a position which I
would not exchange for that of the Turkish sultan, taking
his wealth and giving up my learning. Yea, I would not
exchange it for all the wealth of the world many times multi-
plied; and yet, beyond all doubt, I should not have attained
my present station, if I had not gone to school and learned
to write.

Without anxiety, then, let your son study, and if he should
have to beg bread for a time, you give our God material out
of which he can make a lord. It will remain true that your
son and mine, that is to say, the children of the common
people, will rule the world, both in spiritual and secular
stations, as this Psalm testifies. For wealthy worldings can
not and will not do it; they are the priests and monks of
Mammon, upon whom they are obliged to wait day and
night; princes and lords by birth can not do it alone, and
especially are they unable to fill the spiritual office of the
ministry. Thus must both spiritual and secular government
continue on earth in the hands of the common people and
their children.

And pay no attention to the contempt which the ordinary
devotee of Mammon manifests for culture, so that he says:
"Well, if my son can read, write, and cipher, that is enough;
for I am going to make a merchant out of him?" Without

scholars it would not be long till business men in their per-
plexity would be ready to dig a learned man out of the
ground ten yards deep with their fingers; for the merchant
will not long remain a merchant, if preaching and the administration of justice cease. I know full well that we theologians and jurists must remain, or else all other vocations
will inevitably go to the ground with us; where theologians perish, there perishes also the Word of God, and
nothing but heathen and devils are left; when jurists perish,
there perish also law and peace, and nothing remains but
robbery, murder, outrage, and force—the reign of wild
beasts. But what the merchant will gain when peace van-
ishes, I shall let his ledger tell him; and the use of all his
property when preaching ceases, let his conscience show
him.

It is a ground of special vexation that such foolish and unchristian language is used by those who pretend to be evangelical, and who know how to beat down every opponent
with Scripture; and yet, at the same time, they do not bestow honor enough upon God or their children to educate
them for these divine and exalted offices, through which they
could serve their Maker and the world, and in which their
temporal wants would be provided for. On the contrary,
they turn their children away from these callings, and urge
them to the service of Mammon, in which their success is
uncertain, their bodies and souls are endangered, and their
lives can in no way be considered a service of God.

I should mention here how many learned men are needed
in medicine and the other professions, in reference to which

a book might be written, and six months spent in preaching. Where would our preachers, jurists, and physicians come from, if the liberal arts were not taught? It is from this source they all must come. But to speak of this in detail would carry me too far. To be brief, an industrious, pious school-master or teacher, who faithfully trains and educates boys, can never be sufficiently recompensed, and no money will pay him, as even the heathen Aristotle says. Yet this calling is shamefully despised among us, as if it were nothing —and at the same time we pretend to be Christians!

If I had to give up preaching and my other duties, there is no office I would rather have than that of school-teacher. For I know that next to the ministry it is the most useful, greatest, and best; and I am not sure which of the two is to be preferred. For it is hard to make old dogs docile and old rogues pious, yet that is what the ministry works at, and must work at, in great part, in vain; but young trees, though some may break in the process, are more easily bent and trained. Therefore let it be considered one of the highest virtues on earth faithfully to train the children of others, which duty but very few parents attend to themselves.

That physicians in a sense become lords, is everywhere apparent; and that they can not be dispensed with, is taught by experience; but that medicine is a useful, comforting, and salutary profession, and likewise an acceptable and divinely appointed service of God, appears not only from the work itself, but also from Scripture. The thirty-eighth chapter of Ecclesiasticus is devoted to the praise of physicians: "Honor a physician with the honor due unto him for the uses which you may have of him; for the Lord hath created him. For of the Most High cometh healing. The Lord hath created medicines out of the earth; and he that is wise will not abhor them. Was not the water made sweet with wood, that the virtue thereof might be known? With such doth He heal men, and taketh away their pains. Of such doth the apothecary make a confection; and of his works there is no end," etc. But I am going too far; other preachers may develop these points more fully, and show the people better than I can write it, what injury or benefit may here be done the world and posterity.

Here I will leave the matter, faithfully admonishing and beseeching every one who can to help. For consider how many blessings God has bestowed upon you,—body, soul, house, wife, child, peace, the service and use of all His creatures in heaven and in earth—above all His Gospel and ministry, baptism, the Lord's Supper, and the whole treasure of His Son and Spirit, not only without any merit on your part, but also without cost or labor—and all bestowed in vain; for you support neither schools nor pastors, though according to the Gospel you are under obligation to do so; and besides, you show yourselves such accursed and ungrateful wretches that you are unwilling to give your sons to be educated for maintaining these gifts of God, but possess every thing in vain, not manifesting a drop of gratitude, but on the contrary letting the kingdom of God and the salvation of souls be neglected, to their destruction.

Ought not God to be angry? Ought not famine to come? Ought not pestilence, toil, the French, and other plagues, to find us out? Ought not savage tyrants to reign? Ought not war and strife to arise? Ought not bad government to prevail in the German states? Ought not Turks and Tartars to plunder us? Yea, it would be no wonder if God should open the doors and windows of hell, and let all the devils loose upon us, or if He should rain fire and brimstone from heaven and sink us all in the abyss of hell, as He did Sodom and Gomorrah. For if Sodom and Gomorrah had possessed, and heard, and seen as much as we have been blessed with, they would still exist at the present day. For they were ten times less guilty than Germany is now; for they did not have the Word of God and the ministry as we have them—but alas! in vain, since we act as if we wished that God, His Word, and all discipline and learning, might perish. And indeed factious spirits have actually begun to suppress God's Word, and the nobility and the rich are working to overthrow discipline and honor, that the people may suffer as they have deserved.

To have the Gospel and ministry, what else is it than the blood of our Lord? He secured it and presented it to us through His agonizing death on the cross. Yet we have it in vain, and have done and given nothing for it! O God, how bitterly did He suffer! and yet, how willingly! How much have the dear apostles and all the saints suffered for the Gospel, that it might be transmitted to us! How many in our own time have died for it!

And, to boast a little, how often have I been obliged to suffer the pains of death for the Gospel, that I might serve the German people—but my suffering is nothing in comparison with that of Christ, the Son of God; and yet He receives nothing further from our hands than that some persecute, condemn, and blaspheme this dearly-bought office; while others refuse to support the ministry, and give nothing to maintain that holy office. Moreover, they turn their children away from it, that the office may soon perish, and the sufferings and death of Christ become of no effect; at the same time, they live on in security, feel no compunctions of conscience for their more than diabolical ingratitude and utterly inexpressible sin, exhibit no fear of God's wrath, no love for the dear Saviour on account of His bitter sufferings, and yet, after such frightful wickedness, they pretend to be evangelical Christians!

If this deplorable blindness and sin were to continue in the German states, I should feel sorry that I was born in Germany and that I have spoken and written German; and if I could conscientiously do it, I would advise and help the Pope to rule over us again with all his abominations, and to oppress, flay, and destroy us, even beyond his former tyranny. Formerly, when the devil was served, and Christ's blood insulted, every purse was open, and there was no measure to the contributions made to churches, schools, and every abomination; then, too, people could urge and force their children into cloisters, chapters, churches, schools, with unspeakable cost—all of which was lost.

But now, when good schools and evangelical churches are to be established, nay, not established but merely maintained (for God has already established them, and given sufficient means for their support), when we know that we have God's Word, that evangelical churches are to be maintained, that Christ's sufferings and death are to be honored: now all purses are closed with iron chains, no one can give, and children are not even allowed to be supported by the Church (where nothing is to be given,) and they are prevented from entering such salutary offices, in which their temporal wants would be provided for, and in which they would serve God, and honor the blood of Christ; on the contrary, they are pushed into the jaws of Mammon, they tread the blood of Christ under foot, and yet pretend to be Christians!

I pray God to take me away, that I may never see the sorrow that is to come upon Germany. For I believe that if ten men like Moses stood before God and prayed for us, it would be of no avail; and when I pray for my dear Germany, I feel that my prayer rebounds, and does not ascend to heaven, as it does when I pray for other objects. God grant that I may be a false prophet! These disasters might be averted, if we would reform, and honor the Word of the Lord and the death of Christ as we have not hitherto done, and bring up the young to fill the various offices instituted by God.

But I maintain that the civil authorities are under obligation to compel the people to send their children to school, especially such as are promising, as has elsewhere been said. For our rulers are certainly bound to maintain the spiritual and secular offices and callings, so that there may always be preachers, jurists, pastors, scribes, physicians, school-masters, and the like; for these can not be dispensed with. If the government can compel such citizens as are fit for military service to bear spear and rifle, to mount ramparts, and perform other martial duties in time of war; how much more has it a right to compel the people to send their children to school, because in this case we are warring with the devil, whose object it is secretly to exhaust our cities and principalities of their strong men, to destroy the kernel and leave a shell of ignorant and helpless people, whom he can sport and juggle with at pleasure. That is starving out a city or country, destroying it without a struggle, and without its knowledge. The Turk does differently, and takes every third child in his empire to educate for whatever he pleases. How much more should our rulers require children to be sent to school, who, however, are not taken from their parents, but are educated for their own and the general good, in an office where they have an adequate support.

Therefore, let him who can, watch; and wherever the government sees a promising boy, let him be sent to school. If the father is poor, let the child be aided with the property of the Church. The rich should make bequests to such objects, as some have done, who have founded scholarships; that is giving money to the Church in a proper way. You do not thus release the souls of the dead from purgatorial fire, but you help, through the maintenance of divinely appointed offices, to prevent the living from going to purgatory—yea, you secure their deliverance from hell and entrance into heaven, and bestow upon them temporal peace and happiness. That would be a praise-worthy, Christian bequest, in which God would take pleasure, and for which He would honor and bless you, that you might have joy and peace in Him. Now, my dear Germans, I have warned you enough; you have heard your prophet. God grant that we may follow His Word, to the praise and honor of our dear Lord, for His precious blood so graciously shed for us, and preserve us from the horrible sin of ingratitude and forgetfulness of His benefits. Amen.

AESOP'S FABLES

Aesop's fables had been one of the popular and redeeming texts of the Middle Ages. It was used to teach children morals and Latin. Luther had a lofty appreciation of the value of fables in inculcating good judgment in children and servants. The first passage is taken from the "Table Talk," the other from his Preface to the translation he made of Aesop and published in 1530. The Latin version continued in use for a long time.

The exalted value further attributed to Aesop can be seen in his letter to Melanchthon, Apr. 22, 1530: "We have at last reached our Sinai—but out of this Sinai we shall make a Zion and build three tabernacles: one to the Psalter, one to the Prophets, and one to Aesop."

———

Of the Profit of Esop's Fables

Translated by Capt. Henrie Bell [1]

The Fables of *Esop* (said Luther) ought to bee translated

[1] BELL, CAPT. HENRIE, "Dr. Martin Luther's Divine Discourses at his Table," etc., p. 532.

into High German and brought finely into order; for one man made not that book, but many great people at all times in the world made a part thereof. It is a special Grace of God, that *Cato's* little book, and Fables of *Esop* have been preserved in Schools; for they are both natural and excellent books. *Cato* hath good words and fine precepts which are very profitable in this life. But *Esop* hath excelling sweet *res & picturas*, i. e., matter and the pictures or representations of things. *Ac si meliora adhibeantur adolescentibus, tum multum aedificant,* i. e. and if better things bee read to young men, then they much edify. So far as I am able to understand, next unto the Bible, wee have no better books than *Catonis scripta, & fabulas Aesopi,* the Works of *Cato,* and the Fables of *Esop; Meliora sunt enim scripta ista, quam omnium Philosophorum & Juristarum laceratae sententiae,* for their writings are better than all the tattered sentences of the Philosophers and Lawyers.

About Aesop's Fables [1]

This book of fables and tales has been a celebrated book with the most learned on earth, particularly among the heathen. Though even now, to tell the truth, in speaking of

---

[1] Preface to Aesop's fables translated by Luther in 1530; original in H. Keferstein, "Dr. Martin Luthers Pädagogische Schriften," pp. 3–5.

the outer life in the world, outside of holy writ I do not know many books which should surpass this, if one would consider use, art and wisdom and not just deliberate braying. For one (who knows how to use them) finds therein in the plainest words and simplest fables the very finest lessons, admonition and instruction, as to how one should conduct himself (in domestic affairs) in relation to those in authority and to servants, so that one may live prudently and peaceably among evil people in a false and wicked world. To ascribe the work to Aesop is, in my opinion, a myth, and perhaps there never was a man on earth named Aesop. But I maintain, it was the cooperative work of many wise people assembled piece by piece in time, and finally perhaps put into order by a scholar just as some people may assemble the fables and proverbs now in use in the German tongue, and subsequently somebody will put them in order in a book. For such fine fables all the world could not now invent, not to mention a single individual.

We see that young children and young people are easily moved by fables and tales and are also led with pleasure and love to art and wisdom, which pleasure and love become the greater, if an Aesop or similar masked or carnival figure is presented, who expresses or produces such art that they pay more heed thereto, and receive and retain the same with laughter. But not the children only, but one can beguile also the great princes and lords in no better way to wisdom and its use, than that one have fools speak the truth to them. They can tolerate and listen to them, when they will not or cannot tolerate the truth from any wise person;

in fact all the world hates the truth if it fits them. For this reason such wise and great people have fabricated fables, and have one animal speak with another, as if they would say: Now then! No one will listen to the truth, nor tolerate it, and yet we cannot get on without the truth, so we will deck it out, and dress it in gay, false colors, and delighful fables, and though no one will listen to it from a human mouth, yet they will hear it from the mouths of beasts and animals.

For this reason we have undertaken to clean up this book, and to give it a little better form than it has had, especially for the sake of the youth, that they may learn the more willingly and retain more securely such fine admonitions and lessons, under the delightful form of fables, as in a mummery or play. For we have seen what a clumsy book they have made out of Aesop who have brought to light of day the German Aesop which is here. They well deserve a great punishment because they not only have made such a fine and useful book a disgrace and a useless thing, but also have added much thereto from their own heads. Although this could still be tolerated, yet they have mixed in so much disgraceful and licentious knavery, that no decent and pious man can bear to listen to it in the presence of younger men without feeling ashamed. It is as if they had made a book in the common brothel, or otherwise among loose knaves for they have not sought the good and art in the fables, but have made of them a sport and comedy, just as if wise people had directed great and genuine effort so that senseless people should make a joke and fool's play out of their wisdom. They are swine and remain swine, before whom one should not cast pearls. Therefore we beg all pious hearts to get rid of this disgraceful German Aesop, and use this one in its place. We can, therefore, rejoice and on an evening at table discourse profitably and cheerfully on such fables, without being as scandalous and irrational as in dissolute taverns or inns. For we have worked hard to bring together into this book nothing but good, pure and useful fables after the legend of Aesop. Other useful and harmless fables we will in time, if God wills, purify and cleanse so that it may become a joyful and amiable, but also honorable and decent and useful Aesop that one can laugh at and use without sin to warn and instruct children and servants in regard to their future life and conduct. To this end then it has been edited and published. And that I may give an example, how to use the fables well, if a father wishes to have a useful pastime he can ask his wife, child or servant: What does this or that fable signify? and can exercise himself and them in this way. What does the fifth fable, of the dog with the piece of meat in his mouth, mean: If a servant boy or girl is doing well, but desires something better so he fares as the dog in that he loses the good and does not get the better. Similarly, if a servant hangs on another and is led astray, it goes with him as in the third fable the frog bound to a mouse, which the kite ate together.

Development of Religious Music

Down to the era of the Reformation the music of the church services had always been in Latin, which the common people could not understand. The reformers and especially Luther were aware of the great power of song and took immediate steps to develop hymns which would appeal to the people. These had to be in the vernacular tongues. The first German hymnal appeared in 1524. Luther's celebrated hymn called the "Battle Hymn of the Reformation" is reproduced and some of his statements which indicate what an exalted value he placed upon music.

Luther Promotes German Hymn Writing

Translated by Preserved Smith and Charles M. Jacobs [1]
Luther to Spalatin.

Wittenberg, before January 14, 1524.
Grace and peace. There is a plan afoot to follow the example of the prophets and the fathers of the early Church and compose for the common people German psalms, that is spiritual songs, so that the Word of God may remain among the people in the form of song also. We are seeking everywhere for poets, and since you are gifted with such

[1] "Luther's Correspondence and Other Contemporary Letters," translated and edited by Preserved Smith, Ph.D., and Charles M. Jacobs, D.D., pp. 211–212.

knowledge of the German language and command so elegant a style, cultivated by much use, I beg that you will work with us in this matter and try to translate some one of the psalms into a hymn, like the sample of my own which you have here. But I wish that you would leave out all new words and words that are only used at court. In order to be understood by the people, only the simplest and commonest words should be sung, but they should also be pure and apt and should give a clear sense, as near as possible to that of the Psalter. The translation, therefore, must be free, keeping the sense, but letting the words go and rendering them by other appropriate words. I lack the gift to do what I wish to see done, and so I shall try you and see if you are a Heman [1] or a Asaph [2] or a Jeduthun. [3] I would make the same request of John von Dolzig, whose German is also rich and elegant, but only in case you both have leisure, which I suspect is not the case just now.

You have my Seven Penitential Psalms and the commentaries on them, from which you can get the sense of the psalm, or, if you prefer that a psalm should be assigned to you, I will give you the first, *Domine ne in furore;* or the seventh, *Domine, exaudi orationem;* to Dolzig I will give the second, *Beati quorum,* for I have already translated the *De profundis* and the *Misere mei* has been assigned. If these are too difficult take the two, *Benedicam Dominum in omni tempore* and *Exultate justi in Domino,* that is Psalms 33 and

[1] Psalm 88.
[2] Psalms 73–83.
[3] Psalm 39, etc.

34, or Psalm 103, *Benedice anima mea Dominum*. But tell me what we may hope to have from you. Farewell in the Lord.

Luther's Most Popular Hymn
(1529)

Ein' Feste Burg

A mighty fortress is our God,
A bulwark never failing;
Our helper He, amid the flood
Of mortal ills prevailing.
For still our ancient foe
Doth seek to work us woe;
His craft and pow'r are great,
And, armed with cruel hate,
On earth is not his equal.

Did we in our own strength confide,
Our striving would be losing;
Were not the right man on our side,
The man of God's own choosing.
Dost ask who that may be?
Christ Jesus, it is He;
Lord Sabaoth is His name,
From age to age the same,
And He must win the battle.

And though this world, with devils filled,
Should threaten to undo us,
We will not fear, for God hath willed
His truth to triumph through us.
The Prince of darkness grim,
We tremble not for him;
His rage we can endure,
For lo! his doom is sure:
One little word shall fell him.

158

MARTIN LUTHER

That word above all earthly powers,
No thanks to them, abideth;
The Spirit and the gifts are ours
Through Him who with us sideth
Let goods and kindred go,
This mortal life also;
The body they may kill;
God's truth abideth still,
His Kingdom is forever.

The Value of Music

Translated by Henry Barnard [1]

Music is one of the fairest and best gifts of God; and
Satan hates it, nor can he bear it, since by its means we
exorcise many temptations and wicked thoughts. Music is
one of the best of the arts. The notes breathe life into the
words. It chases away the spirit of melancholy, as we may
see by the case of King Saul. Some of our nobility think that
they have done some great thing, when they give three thousand gulden yearly toward music, and yet they will throw
away, without scruple, perhaps, thirty thousand on follies.
Kings, princes and lords must maintain music (for it is the
duty of great potentates and monarchs to uphold excellent,
liberal arts, as well as laws), inasmuch as the common people and private individuals desire it, and would have it if

[1] BARNARD, HENRY, "German Teachers and Educators," pp.
158–159, translated from Karl von Raumer, "Geschichte der
Pädagogik," Vol. I, pp. 143–145. Original in Georg Walch,
"Luthers sämtliche Schriften," Vol. XXII, pp. 2249–2253. Compare Preserved Smith, and Herbert Percival Gallinger, "Conver-
sations with Luther," pp. 98–100.

their means were sufficient. Music is the best solace to a wearied man; through it, the heart is again quieted, quickened, and refreshed; as that one says, in Virgil:

Tu calamos inflare leves, ego dicere versus.

Do you play the air, and I will sing the verse.

Music is a half-discipline, and it is a teacher; it makes men gentler and milder, more mannerly and more rational. And even poor violinists or organists do us this service, they show us what a noble and excellent art music is, as we can distinguish white the better if we place black beside it.

On the 17th of December, 1538, while Dr. M. Luther was entertaining some musicians at his house, who sang many sweet tunes and lofty cantatas, he exclaimed, in his rapture: "If in this life our Lord God has scattered around and heaped upon us such noble gifts, what will it be in that immortal life, where all is perfection and fullness of delight? But here we have only the beginning, the *materia prima*. I have always loved music. He who knows this art is in the right frame, and fitted for every good pursuit. We can not do without music in our schools. A schoolmaster must know how to sing, or I would not allow him to teach. Nor ought we to ordain young theologians to the sacred office, unless they have first been well-tried and practiced in the art in the school." As they sang a cantata of Senffel's, Luther was filled with emotion and wonder, praising it highly. He then said: "Such a cantata it is not in my power to compose, even though I should try to my utmost; nor, on the other hand, could Senffel expound a psalm as well as I. For the gifts of the Holy Spirit are of divers kinds; so in one body there are different members. But no one is contented with his own gift, no one rests satisfied with what God has bestowed upon him, for all wish to be, not members merely, but the whole body.

"Music is a fair, glorious gift of God; and it lies very near to theology. I would not part with my small faculty of music for vast possessions. We should practice the young continually in this art, for it will make able and polished men of them.

"Singing is the best art and exercise. It has nothing in common with the world; it is far-removed from the jar and wrangling of the court and the lawsuit. Singers, too, are never overwhelmed with care, but are joyful; and, with their singing, they drive care out and away."

And he said further: "How comes it to pass that, in carnal things, we have so many a fine poem, and so many a sweet song, while, in spiritual things, all is so cold and listless?" He then recited some German odes, "The Tournament," by Bollen, etc. "I hold this to be the reason, as St. Paul has expressed it, in Romans, 7: 23; 'I see another law warring in my members,' a law that will not be overcome, and that does not yield up its power so readily as does the law in the soul. If any one despises music, as all the fanatics do, I can not confide in him. For music is a gift and bestowment of God; it does not proceed from man. And it drives away the devil, and makes men happy: in it, we forget all anger, lasciviousness, pride, and every vice. Next to theology I rank music, and hold it in almost equal honor. For look how David and all holy men have uttered their heavenly meditations in verse, rhyme and song. *Quia pacis tempore regnat musica.*"

THE CURRICULA OF THE SCHOOLS

The remaining passages from Luther's writings deal with the subjects he wished taught in the schools. Unlike the former passages they are not placed in chronological order of composition. One will have already noted in many places the great emphasis he placed upon the acquisition of languages. Much as he accomplished in making the High German dialect the classical German tongue, we do not find that he appreciated the study of the vernacular. In the Saxon school ordinance [1] which he approved as the new school system, all languages except Latin were expressly excluded. Luther, elsewhere, commended the study of Greek and Hebrew. Probably he expected these languages to be learned as university studies, or in the schools of the larger cities.

Summing up Luther's idea of the curriculum it would include religion, music, Latin grammar, Aesop's "Fables," Latin literature of a limited scope, Latin plays, rhetoric, dialectic, mathematics, Ptolemaic astronomy,[2] ethics, physics, theology, history, Greek, and Hebrew. He had no interest in humanistic studies, nor

[1] See below, pp. 180–187.
[2] Luther vigorously rejected the Copernican theory as contrary to the Scriptures.

is there much indication that he was awake to the natural sciences which were at that time in their infancy.

The Study of Grammar

Translated by Henry Barnard [1]

The art of grammar teaches and shows, what words imply and signify; but we must first learn and know what the things are, and what the matters mean. Hence, must he, who would teach and preach, first know his subject and its bearing, before he can speak of it; for grammar only teaches the names and forms of the words which we use to set forth our subject.

Our knowledge is two-fold; relating to words on the one hand, and on the other to things. And accordingly, he who does not possess a knowledge of the thing or the subject of which he is to speak, will not find a knowledge of words of any service to him. There is an old proverb, which runs thus: If you do not know what you are talking of, you may talk forever, and no man will be the wiser. Many such people there are in our day. For we have many very learned and very eloquent men, who appear exceedingly foolish and ridiculous, because they undertake to speak of that which they have never understood.

But, whoever has the matter inwrought into his being, so that he comprehends it fully, is an able teacher, and reaches

[1] BARNARD, HENRY, "German Teachers and Educators," pp. 154–155, translated from Karl von Raumer, "Geschichte der Pädagogik," Vol. I, pp. 138–139. Original in Georg Walch, "Luthers sämtliche Schriften," Vol. XXII, p. 2245.

the heart, whether he be eloquent, and have a ready flow of words, or not. So Cato, when he spoke in the council, had more influence than Cicero, albeit, his language was rough and devoid of all polish and elegance; and, though his speech was not skillfully framed to produce conviction, yet no one ever gave a thought to his manner.

Accordingly, the understanding of words, or grammar, is easy, when we well understand the subject; as Horace also says: that words come of their own accord, when the subject has been duly admitted to the mind, retained there, and fully considered; but, where the subject is obscurely apprehended, there the utmost knowledge of words will do no good. I have dwelt upon this point so fully for this reason, namely: that you may know, if you shall ever read the Rabbins, what sort of masters you will have; they may well understand the language, but the subjects that are conveyed in it they know nothing about, nor can they ever teach them in a true and proper manner.

But, through the goodness and the grace of God, we have the knowledge and the understanding of the matters, of which the Holy Scriptures treat, while they are left in blindness. Hence, though they know the grammar, yet they have no correct understanding of the Scriptures; but, as Isaiah, (29, 11,) saith: "And the vision is become as the words of a book that is sealed. Who then shall follow them?"

Now let no one think or conclude from all this that I would reject the grammar, for this is altogether necessary; but this much I do say: he who, with the grammar, does not study the contents of the Scriptures also, will never make a good teacher. For, as a certain one has said, "the words of the teacher or preacher should follow the subject, and grow, not in his mouth, but out of his heart."

Methods of Learning Languages

Translated by Henry Barnard [1]

.   .   .   .

We learn German or other languages much better by word of mouth, at home, in the street, or at the church, than out of books. Letters are dead words; the utterances of the mouth are living words, which in writing can never stand forth so distinct and so excellent, as the soul and spirit of man bodies them forth through the mouth.

Tell me, where was there ever a language, which men could learn to speak with correctness and propriety by the rules of grammar? Is it not true that even those languages, like the Latin and the Greek, which possess the most unerring rules, are much better learned by use and wont, than from these rules? Is it not then extremely absurd, for one who would learn the sacred tongue, in which divine and spiritual things are discoursed of, to neglect a straightforward and pertinent search into the subject-matter and attempt, instead, to pick the language out of grammar alone?

[1] BARNARD, HENRY, "German Teachers and Educators," p. 154, translated from Karl von Raumer, "Geschichte der Pädagogik," Vol. I, p. 137. Original in Georg Walch, "Luthers sämtliche Schriften," Vol. III, p. 2867, and Vol. I, p. 683.

Of Languages

Translated by Capt. Henrie Bell [1]

LUTHER'S DISCOURS OF LANGUAGES

The wisdom of the *Grecians,* in comparison of the wisdom of the Jews, is altogether Beastial, for without God, no wisdom nor true understanding can bee, the wisdom of the *Grecians* consisteth in an external virtuous and civil conversation, but the end of the wisdom of the Jews (such as are upright good and Godly) is to fear God and to trust in him. The wisdom of the world is the wisdom of the *Grecians,* from whence *Daniel* nameth all the Kingdoms of the world (according to their kindes) Beasts and ignorant Cattle, the *Grecians* have good and pleasing words, but not sentences, their language is amiable and of a courteous kinde, but not rich of sentences. The Hebrew tongue above other languages is very plain, but therewith it is majestical and glorious, it conteineth much in simple and few words, and therein surpasseth all other languages. The Hebrew tongue is the best and richest in words, it is a pure language, which neither beggeth nor borroweth of others, shee hath her own proper color, Greek, Latin and the *German* tongue do beg of others, they have many *Composita,* that is, words set together or compounded words, as for example, where

[1] BELL, CAPT. HENRIE, Dr. Martin Luther's "Divine Discourses at His Table," etc., pp. 501–502.

the *Germans* have one single or simple word, so have they at the least twentie compounded words issuing thereout, as *laufen* (in English, to run) they have, *belauffen, inlauffen, ablauffen, wegklaffen, umblauffen, emlauffen,* etc. But the Hebrew hath no compounded but a proper word for the same; the Hebrew tongue (after the Babilonian captivitie) fell away in such sort, that never since it could again bee brought to perfection, but for the most part they speak the *Caldean* language, yet corrupted, mingled and unpure, as the *Walloons* speak Latin. Languages of themselvs (said *Luther*) make not a Divine, they are onely helps unto him, for when one intendeth to speak of a thing, so ought hee before to know and understand the business, for my part I use the common *German* tongue, to the end both high and low Countrie people may understand mee, I speak according to the *Saxonian* Chancerie, which is imitated in the Courts of all *German* princes, insomuch that it is the general *German* language. *Maximilian* the Emperor, and *Frederick* Prince Elector of *Saxon,* drew the *German* tongue into the *Roman* Empire. I learned more Hebrew (said *Luther*) when in reading I compared one place and sentence with another, then when I directed the same upon and towards the Grammar. If I were young, so would I contrive a waie and means for the perfect learning of the Hebrew tongue, which is both glorious and profitable, and without which the Holie Scriptures cannot rightly bee understood, for although the new Testament bee written in Greek, yet it is full of the Hebrew kinde of speaking, from whence it is truly said, *The He-*

brews drink out of the Fountain, but the Grecians out of the Springs that flow from the Fountain, the Latins out of the Pits. I am no Hebrew according to the Grammar rules, for I permit not my self to bee tied, but go freely thorough, when although one have the gift of languages and understandeth them, yet hee cannot so soon bring one into another well to translate them. To translate, is a special gift and Grace of God. The seventie *Grecian* Interpreters that translated the Hebrew Bible into Greek, were unexperienced and unpractised in the Hebrew language, their translations are very doultish and impertinent, for they contemned the Letters, the words and manner of speaking, insomuch that the translation and Interpretation of *Hieronimus* is to bee preferred before them, yet nevertheless whoso nick nameth *Hieronimus* and calleth him an Hebrew, the same doth him much wrong. I am perswaded (said *Luther*) that if *Moses* and the Prophets should now arise again, so would they not understand their own words and language, as now the same are screwed. Even so, the Latin tongue was spoiled by the *Goth's,* insomuch that *Cicero,* and others who lived in their times, would not understand their own mother tongue, if now they were again alive. *Lyra* (said *Luther*) above all others was the best *Hebrician* or Hebrew, and a diligent translator of the old and new Testaments. Hee that will studie in the Hebrew tongue, let him take the purest and best *Grammaticos,* as *David Kimchi* and *Moses Kunckey* which are the best and purest, afterwards let him read *Moses,* in regard hee speaketh altogether properly concerning things, then let him read also the Psalter and the Proverbs of

Solomon, and at last, let him read the Prophets, who use many colored speeches and words.

THAT THE TONGUE IS THE INSTRUMENT OF SPEAKING

The tongues of mankinde, are wonderful works and creations of God, which are able to shew the words significantly, distinct and apprehensivly, every Countrie hath his particular kinde of language and speaking; the *Grecians* pronounce the letter (R) onely in the Throat, with an (H) insomuch as it was a very difficult and hard matter, for *Demosthenes* (the most eloquent speaker in the Greek tongue) to pronounce this (R) without rattling in the Throat, yet at last practise overcame nature, so that hee was able plainly to pronounce it. For the superfluitie of the moistness of the Brain hindereth the tongue, as wee see on the drunken bolts. Thus God gave to his creature (mankinde) a working Toole.

No language (said *Luther*) hath so many colored and figured words, as the Hebrew. In *St. Peters* Epistle is almost no proper word. *Moses* and *David* wrote plain and simply, *Solomon* doth quite contrarie. The Grecians have many *propria,* that is, own significant words.

As I took in hand to translate the Bible into High Dutch, I gave and perscribed those rules which help mee (said *Luther*); *first,* the Holie Scripture speaketh of Divine works and things, *secondly,* when a sentence and meaning agreeth with the new Testament, then to accept thereof, *thirdly,* that the Grammar bee well regarded.

Logic and Rhetoric Compared

Translated by Henry Barnard [1]

Logic is a lofty art; it speaks direct, whether of wrong or right, as if I should say, "give me some drink." But rhetoric adds ornament, as thus: "give me of the pleasant juice in the cellar, the curling, sparkling juice, that makes the heart merry."

Logic tells us *how* to teach everything; still, for all this, though we have learned it so that we thoroughly understand it, it does not, of itself, give us the *ability* to teach anything; for it is only an instrument and a tool, by means of which we may impart, in a correct and methodical manner, that which we already understand and know. For instance, I can not speak of mining or of the duties of the overseer of a mine, because I neither know how to open a mine, nor how to sink a shaft, nor can I tell where the galleries should run; but, had I searched into this matter, and become familiar with it, I should then be better able to speak on the subject than the surveyor himself. Logic does not furnish the subject of which we are to speak, or the branch that we are to teach; it only directs us how to teach such branch, or to speak of such subject, in a just and appropriate manner, with method, directness, and brevity.

Logic is a useful and a necessary art, which we ought with

---

[1] BARNARD, HENRY, "German Teachers and Educators," p. 157, translated from Karl von Raumer, "Geschichte der Pädagogik," Vol. I, pp. 141–142. Compare William Hazlitt, "The Table Talk of Martin Luther," pp. 339–340, 1902.

as much reason to study and to learn as we do arithmetic or geometry. And, though there are some heads so sharp by nature, that they can draw conclusions and form judgments, on almost any subject, from the impressions they receive from it, yet this is an uncertain and a dangerous gift, unless art come to its aid. For logic gives us a clear, correct, and methodical arrangement, showing us the grounds of our conclusions, and how we may know, to a certainty, from the nature of the subject itself, what is right or wrong, and what we should judge and decide.

Logic teaches, rhetoric moves and persuades; the latter controls the will, the former the understanding. St. Paul includes them both, in Romans, 12: 7, 8: "He that teacheth, let him wait on teaching; or he that exhorteth, on exhortation."

The most excellent fruit and use of logic is to define and describe a thing with completeness and brevity, and, in accordance with its nature, neither more nor less than it is. Hence, we should accustom ourselves to use good, pointed, and intelligible words, words that are in common use, and thereby fitted to call up and set forth the matter, so that men may understand just what it includes. And, if any man has this power, let him give God the glory, for it is a special gift and grace, since crafty writers often disguise their sentiments designedly, with astonishing, far-fetched, or obsolete words; inventing a new style and mode of speaking, so double-sided, double-tongued, and intertangled, that, when convenient, they can bend their language into whatever meaning they choose, as the heretics do.

Eloquence does not consist in a tinseled flourish of gaudy and unfamiliar words, but in that chaste and polished expression, which, like a beautiful painting, shows the subject-matter in a clear, suitable and every way admirable light. They who coin and foist in strange words, must also bring in strange and novel things, as did Scotus, with his "hiccity," "nominality," etc., or the Anabaptists, with their "immersion," "purification," "quietism," etc. Hence, you should beware, above all things, of those who make frequent use of new, unfamiliar and useless words; for such a mode of speaking is at war with all true eloquence.

On the Value of History

Translated by Henry Barnard [1]

Says the highly-renowned Roman, Varro, (so this preface runs,) the best instruction is that which combines illustration and example with precept. For through these we apprehend the speech or the doctrine more clearly, and also retain it the more readily in our memories; but, where the discourse is without illustration, no matter how just and ex-

[1] BARNARD, HENRY, "German Teachers and Educators," pp. 155–156, translated from Karl von Raumer, "Geschichte der Pädagogik," Vol. I, pp. 139–141. Original, Preface to Galeatti Capella's "History of the Duke of Milan," "D. Martin Luthers Werke," Weimar ed., Vol. 50, pp. 383–385; also Georg Walch, "Luthers sämtliche Schriften," Vol. XIV, pp. 354–358.

cellent it may be in itself, yet it does not move the heart with such power, neither is it so clear, nor so easily remembered. Hence, we may see what a priceless value resides in histories. For all that philosophers, sages, and the collective wisdom of humanity can devise or teach, relative to the conduct of life, this, history, with her incidents and examples, enforces, causing it all to pass before our eyes, so to speak, as if we ourselves were on the spot, beholding those things in action, whose nature we had heard before in doctrine or in precept. There we learn what things those who were pious and wise pursued, what they shunned, and how they lived, and how it fared with them, or how they were rewarded; and again, how they lived who were wicked and obstinate in their ignorance, and what punishments overtook them.

And did we but think of it, all laws, arts, good counsels, warnings, threatenings, terrors,—all solace, strength, instruction, foresight, wisdom, prudence, together with every virtue, —flow from records and histories as from a living fountain. For histories are an exhibition, memorial, and monument of the works and the judgments of God; how he upholds and rules the world, and men more than all, causing their plans to prosper or to fail, lifting them on high, or humbling them in the dust, according as their deeds are good or evil. And though there be many who neither know nor regard God, yet even such can not fail to start back before the portraitures of history, and to fear lest the same evils come upon them, too, that overtook this or that person, whose course is graven, as a warning, forever upon the page of history; whereby they will be far more deeply moved, than if you should strive to restrain and curb them with the bare letter of the law, or with mere dry doctrine. So we read, not in the Holy Scriptures alone, but in pagan books too, how the men of old instanced and held up to view the example of their forefathers, in word and in deed, when they wished to arouse the enthusiasm of the people, or when on any occasion they would teach and admonish, or warn and deter.

Hence, too, historians are the most useful of men, and the best of teachers. Nor can we ever accord too much praise, honor, or gratitude to them; and it should be the work of the great ones of the earth, as emperors, kings, and the like, to cause a faithful record to be made of the history of their own times, and to have such records sacredly preserved and set in order in libraries. And, to this end, they should spare no expense, which may be needful, to educate and maintain those persons whose talents mark them out for this task.

But he who would write history, must be a superior man, —lion-hearted and fearless in writing truth. For most manage to pass by in silence, or at least to gloss over the vices or the mischances of their times, to please great lords or their own friends; or they give too high a place to minor, or it may be, insignificant actions; or else, from an overweening love of country, and a hatred toward foreign nations, they bedizen or befoul histories, according to their own likes or dislikes. Hence it is, that a suspicious air invests histories, and God's providence is shamefully obscured; so the Greeks did in their perverseness, so the Pope's flatterers have done heretofore, and are now doing, till it has come to this, at last, that we do not know what to admit or what to reject. Thus the noble, precious, and highest use of history is overlooked, and we have only a vain babble and gossip. And this is because the worthy task of writing annals and records is open to every one without discrimination; and they write or slur over, praise or condemn, at their will.

How important, then, is it, that this office should be filled by men of eminence, or at least by those who are worthy. For, inasmuch as histories are records of God's work, that is, of his grace and his displeasure, which men should believe with as much reason as if the same stood written in the Bible, surely they ought to be penned with all diligence, truth and fidelity. This, however, will, I fear, never come to pass, unless the enactment which was in force with the Jews shall again bear sway. Meanwhile, we must rest content with our histories as they are, and reflect and judge for ourselves, as we peruse them, whether the writer has been warped through favor or prejudice, whether he praises or blames either too little or too much, according as the persons or the events that come under his notice, please or displease him; just as in such a loose government as ours, we must endure to have carriers dilute their foreign wine with water, so that we can not buy the pure growth, but must content ourselves with getting some part pure, be this more or be it less.

EARLY PROTESTANT EDUCATORS

Physical Exercise

Translated by Henry Barnard [1]

.   .   .   .

It was admirably provided and ordered by the ancients that the people should have honorable and useful modes of exercise to resort to, so that they might not fall into gluttony, lewdness, surfeiting, rioting, and gambling. Accordingly, I pronounce in favor of these two exercises and pastimes, namely, music, and the knightly sports of fencing, wrestling, etc., of which, the one drives care and gloom from the heart, and the other gives a full development to the limbs, and maintains the body in health. And another argument for them is this, that they keep men from tippling, lewdness, cards, and dice, which, alas! are now so common everywhere, at court and in the town, where we hear nothing but "fair play!" "more wine!" and the like phrases. And then, in their flush, they stake you, perhaps, an hundred gulden or more, at a cast. So it goes, when those other honorable exercises and knightly sports are scorned and neglected.

[1] BARNARD, HENRY, "German Teachers and Educators," p. 158, translated from Karl von Raumer, "Geschichte der Pädagogik," Vol. I, pp. 142, 143. Original in Georg Walch, "Luthers sämtliche Schriften," Vol. XXII, p. 2247.

PHILIP MELANCHTHON

Praeceptor Germaniae

LIFE AND WORK

PHILIP MELANCHTHON, invariably honored with the title *Praeceptor Germaniae,* was the confidant and coworker of Luther not alone as religious reformer but also as educational rebuilder. He was the greater scholar and more directly concerned with the practical reorganization of the secondary schools and universities. Born in 1497, he was a very precocious youth, graduating from Heidelberg before fifteen years of age. In 1518 he was appointed to teach Greek at Wittenberg, where, as it will be recalled, Luther was just beginning his revolt against the Catholic Church. His great classical learning soon gained him a widening influence in the higher schools. With Luther, Bugenhagen, and others he engaged in the church and school survey in 1527 and 1528. The recommendations for reforming conditions which resulted from this survey were the work of Melanchthon, though the document was passed around for revision and was also published among Luther's writings. After the first visitation in the principality of Saxony other states were visited in a similar manner and with like results.

The "Book of Visitation" contains the school plan which is given below. It recommends that schools to teach Latin only be established. The exclusion of Greek is interesting; the prohibition against vernacular schools is in sharpest contrast to the early vision of Luther on the one hand and the practical course of Bugenhagen in founding elementary German schools for boys and for girls. This limitation of the curriculum to the Latin language was not intended for the larger town schools.

Melanchthon's great service for education lay especially in two lines, in the counsel and personal help he gave in organizing and in directing the Latin schools in many places; and in his work in assisting in the reorganization of the curricula of the universities. Unfortunately work of this character does not always come in the form of source material. Only the "School Plan" is selected for inclusion here. The students should compare this three-class plan of Melanchthon with the more elaborate Latin schools of Sturm and Calvin.

BOOK OF VISITATION SCHOOL PLAN

Translated by Henry Barnard [1]

Concerning Schools

Preachers also should exhort the people of their charge to send their children to school, so that they may be trained up to teach sound doctrine in the church, and to serve the state in a wise and able manner. Some imagine that it is enough for a teacher to understand German. But this is a

[1] BARNARD, HENRY, "German Teachers and Educators," pp. 169-171, translated from Karl von Raumer, "Geschichte der Pädagogik," Vol. I, pp. 155-158; Reinhold Vorbaum, "'Evangelische Schulordnungen," Vol. I, pp. 1-8.

misguided fancy. For he, who is to teach others, must have great practice and special aptitude; to gain this, he must have studied much, and from his youth up. For St. Paul tells us, in 1 Tim., 3: 2, that a bishop must be "apt to teach." And herein he would have us infer that bishops must possess this quality in greater measure than laymen. So also he commends Timothy, (1 Tim., 4: 6), in that he has learned from his youth up, having been "nourished up in the words of faith, and of good doctrine." For this is no small art, namely, to teach and direct others in a clear and correct manner, and it is impossible that unlearned men should attain to it. Nor do we need able and skillful persons for the church alone, but for the government of the world too; and God requires it at our hands. Hence parents should place their children at school, in order there to arm and equip them for God's service, so that God can use them for the good of others.

But in our day there are many abuses in children's schools. And it is that these abuses may be corrected, and that the young may have good instruction, that we have prepared this plan. In the first place, the teachers must be careful to teach the children Latin only, not German, nor Greek, nor Hebrew, as some have heretofore done, burdening the poor children with such a multiplicity of pursuits, that are not only unproductive, but positively injurious. Such schoolmasters, we plainly see, do not think of the improvement of the children at all, but undertake so many languages solely to increase their own reputation. In the second place, teachers should not burden the children with too many books, but should rather avoid a needless variety. Thirdly, it is indispensable that the children be classified into distinct groups.

The First Group.—The first group should consist of those children who are learning to read. With these the following method is to be adopted: They are first to be taught the child's-manual, containing the alphabet, the creed, the Lord's prayer, and other prayers. When they have learned this, Donatus and Cato may both be given them; Donatus for a reading book, and Cato they may explain after the following manner: the schoolmaster must give them the explanation of a verse or two, and then in a few hours call upon them to repeat what he has thus said; and in this way they will learn a great number of Latin words, and lay up a full store of phrases to use in speech. In this they should be exercised until they can read well. Neither do we consider it time lost, if the feebler children, who are not especially quick-witted, should read Cato and Donatus not once only, but a second time. With this they should be taught to write, and be required to shew their writing to the schoolmaster every day. Another mode of enlarging their knowledge of Latin words is to give them every afternoon some words to commit to memory, as has been the custom in schools hitherto. These children must likewise be kept at music, and be made to sing with the others, as we shall show, God willing, further on.

The Second Group.—The second group consists of children who have learned to read, and are now ready to go into grammar. With these the following regulations should be observed: The first hour after noon every day all the children, large and small, should be practiced in music. Then the schoolmaster must interpret to the second group the fables of Aesop. After vespers, he should explain to them the "Paedology" of Mosellanus; and, when this is finished, he should select from the "Colloquies" of Erasmus some that may conduce to their improvement and discipline. This should be repeated on the next evening also. When the children are about to go home for the night, some short sentence may be given them, taken perhaps from a poet, which they are to repeat the next morning, such as *Amicus certus in re incerta cernitur.*—A true friend becomes manifest in adversity. Or *Fortuna, quem nimium fovet, stultum facit.*—Fortune, if she fondles a man too much, makes him a fool. Or this from Ovid: *Vulgus amicitias utilitate probat.* —The rabble value friendships by the profit they yield.

In the morning the children are again to explain Aesop's fables. With this the teacher should decline some nouns or verbs, many or few, easy or difficult, according to the progress of the children, and then ask them the rules and the reasons for such inflection. And at the same time when they shall have learned the rules of construction, they should be required to *construe,* (parse,) as it is called; this is a very useful exercise, and yet there are not many who employ it. After the children have thus learned Aesop, Terence is to be given to them; and this they must commit to memory, for they will now be older, and able to work harder. Still the master must be cautious, lest he overtask them. Next after

Terence, the children may take hold of such of the comedies of Plautus as are harmless in their tendency, as the "Aulularia," the "Trinummus," the "Pseudolus," etc.

The hour before mid-day must be invariably and exclusively devoted to instruction in grammar: first etymology, then syntax, and lastly prosody. And when the teacher has gone thus far through with the grammar, he should begin it again, and so on continually, that the children may understand it to perfection. For if there is negligence here, there is neither certainty nor stability in whatever is learned beside. And the children should learn by heart and repeat all the rules, so that they may be driven and forced, as it were, to learn the grammar well.

If such labor is irksome to the schoolmaster, as we often see, then we should dismiss him, and get another in his place,—one who will not shrink from the duty of keeping his pupils constantly in the grammar. For no greater injury can befall learning and the arts, than for youth to grow up in ignorance of grammar.

This course should be repeated daily, by the week together; nor should we by any means give children a different book to study each day. However, one day, for instance, Sunday or Wednesday, should be set apart, in which the children may receive Christian instruction. For some are suffered to learn nothing in the Holy Scriptures; and some masters there are who teach children nothing but the Scriptures; both of which extremes must be avoided. For it is essential that children be taught the rudiments of the Christian and divine life. So likewise there are many reasons why, with the Scriptures, other books too should be laid before them, out of which they may learn to read. And in this matter we propose the following method: Let the schoolmaster hear the whole group, making them, one after the other, repeat the Lord's prayer, the creed, and the ten commandments. But if the group is too large, it may be divided, so that one week one part may recite, and the remaining part the next.

After one recitation, the master should explain in a simple and correct manner the Lord's prayer, after the next the creed, and at another time the ten commandments. And he should impress upon the children the essentials, such as the fear of God, faith, and good works. He must not touch upon polemics, nor must he accustom the children to scoff at monks or any other persons, as many unskillful teachers use to do.

With this the schoolmaster may give the boys some plain psalms to commit to memory, which comprehend the sum and substance of the Christian life, which inculcate the fear of the Lord, faith, and good works. As the 112th Psalm, "Blessed is the man that feareth the Lord"; the 34th, "I will bless the Lord at all times"; the 128th, "Blessed is every one that feareth the Lord, that walketh in His ways"; the 125th, "They that trust in the Lord shall be as Mount Zion, which can not be removed, but abideth forever"; the 127th, "Except the Lord build the house, they labor in vain that build it"; the 133d, "Behold how good and how pleasant it is for brethren to dwell together in unity!" or other such plain and intelligible psalms, which likewise should be expounded in the briefest and most correct manner possible, so that the children may know, both the substance of what they have learned and where to find it.

On this day too the teacher should give a grammatical exposition of Matthew; and, when he has gone through with it, he should commence it anew. But, when the boys are somewhat more advanced, he may comment upon the two epistles of Paul to Timothy, or the 1st Epistle of John, or the Proverbs of Solomon. But teachers must not undertake any other books. For it is not profitable to burden the young with deep and difficult books as some do, who, to add to their own reputation, read Isaiah, Paul's Epistle to the Romans, St. John's Gospel, and others of a like nature.

The Third Group.—Now, when these children have been well trained in grammar, those among them who have made the greatest proficiency should be taken out, and formed into the third group. The hour after mid-day they, together with the rest, are to devote to music. After this the teacher is to give an explanation of Virgil. When he has finished this, he may take up Ovid's "Metamorphoses," and in the latter part of the afternoon Cicero's "Offices," or "Letters to Friends." In the morning Virgil may be reviewed, and the teachers, to keep up practice in the grammar, may call for constructions and inflections, and point out the prominent figures of speech.

The hour before mid-day, grammar should still be kept up, that the scholars may be thoroughly versed therein. And when they are perfectly familiar with etymology and syntax, then prosody (*metrica*) should be opened to them, so that they can thereby become accustomed to make verses. For this exercise is a very great help toward understanding the writings of others; and it likewise gives the boys a rich fund of words, and renders them accomplished many ways. In course of time, after they have been sufficiently practiced in the grammar, this same hour is to be given to logic and rhetoric. The boys in the second and third groups are to be required every week to write compositions, either in the form of letters or of verses. They should also be rigidly confined to Latin conversation, and to this end the teachers themselves must, as far as possible, speak nothing but Latin with the boys; thus they will acquire the practice by use, and the more rapidly for the incentives held out to them.

JOHANN BUGENHAGEN

BIOGRAPHICAL NOTE

JOHANN BUGENHAGEN was born in 1485 in Pomerania which lies on the north central coast of Germany. He studied philosophy, theology, and the classics at the University of Greifswald and at the age of eighteen took charge of a classical school. In 1520 he became a Protestant and associated himself with Luther and Melanchthon at Wittenberg where he was appointed to the chair of theology and pastor of the town church. More than either Luther or Melanchthon he was the practical organizer of the Reformation. His special sphere of activity, however, lay in the towns and principalities of northern Germany and Denmark where he was most at home. He took part in the church and school visitation in 1527 and was deeply interested in promoting schools in the cities of Brunswick, Hamburg, Lübeck, Bremen, in the principalities of Pomerania and Schleswig-Holstein, and in the Kingdom of Denmark. In the Hanseatic towns several centuries earlier a movement had taken place for the establishment of Latin schools and also German schools for the teaching of reading and writing to the children of the rising commercial class. Those schools taught only the secular arts and were greatly disliked by the various church schools. Into the old root Bugenhagen sought to graft a new order, a system of Latin and vernacular schools under the control of the city authorities in which the Protestant religion was taught together with the secular subjects. Due to the favorable conditions which existed in this part of the country, the city councils were willing to establish some town schools for boys and separate schools for girls in which the vernacular was used; also Latin schools for the higher class of students. This portion of Germany anticipated southern German states at least a generation or more in the founding of such popular schools. It is, one must note, a mistake to conceive that any of the church reformers zealously advocated vernacular elementary schools except for purely religious instruction. Careful study of the section dealing with German schools in the school ordinance which follows and of the others to be found later on will show that this type of schools was regarded as quite unimportant.

Bugenhagen worked through the cities and principalities by the adoption of church ordinances which contained sections dealing with the founding of schools. This was by no means a new method, for such church school ordinances had been common for a long time. Only part of the church ordinance dealing with the town of Brunswick is offered here. It was somewhat hurriedly written by Bugenhagen in 1528 and was typical. Other ordinances of the same character were written by him for Hamburg, 1529; Lübeck, 1531; Bremen, 1534; Pomerania, 1535; Schleswig-Holstein, 1542; Brunswick-Wolfenbüttel, 1543; and Denmark and Norway still later. Bugenhagen died in 1558; his services to popular education were greater in practical results than those of either Luther or Melanchthon.

JOHANN BUGENHAGEN

School Ordinance from the Church Ordinance of the Town of Brunswick [1]

(1528)

Concerning the Schools

Before all else, therefore, it is considered necessary here at Brunswick through the honorable council and the entire community to establish good schools and to employ honorable, well-grounded, scholarly masters and assistants to the honor of God the Almighty for the welfare of the youth and the satisfaction of the entire city. Therein the poor, ignorant youth may be properly trained, learn the ten commandments, the creed, the Lord's prayer, the Christian sacraments, with as much of explanation as is suitable for children, also learn to sing the psalms in Latin, and read passages every day from the Latin scriptures. In addition they are to study the humanities from which one learns to understand such matters. And not merely that, but also that in time there may come good schoolmasters, good preachers, good jurists, good physicians, God-fearing, decent, honorable, well-grounded, obedient, sociable, scholarly, peaceable, sober but happy citizens, who henceforth may train their children in the best way, and so on the children's children.

This will God have from us, he will also be with us through his grace, that this may take place and be successful.

[1] Translated from original in Friedrich Koldewey, "Braunschweigische Schulordnungen," "Monumenta Germaniae Paedagogica," Vol. I, pp. 27–38.

The Jews taught their children in the homes, and had schools in every town, which were called synagogues, so that they learned well the law of Moses, and could defend their faith. Furthermore, the Jews still teach their children in their own way. Among us Christians it is certainly disgraceful that we do not learn to know Christ rightly in whom we are baptized; furthermore it is a shame that we do not have the youth taught such arts as will help them to be of service to themselves and to the world, and serviceable to the salvation of their souls and to the good government in these lands and cities.

If our industry does not succeed with some children, it will with many others. A tree that bears many good apples, should not be hewn down because two or three are wormy. We must not neglect to do good, because it is thrown away on some individuals.

Latin Elementary Schools

Two good elementary Latin schools are considered sufficient, and although this is few enough in such a city, nevertheless you will maintain the two schools the more creditably and diligently with learned masters and assistants so that the youth may be well provided for.

The one school shall be at St. Martin's Church. There you will maintain one learned master of arts, to the honor of the city and the welfare of the youth. For although at first little children do not require a great master, as it would seem, nevertheless learned and experienced masters with better method can teach gifted children more with the help of God in three years or in even a shorter time than others in twenty. If one attempts it, one will succeed with some children. Furthermore such a man can be very useful if anything occurs that concerns the gospel, and likewise he can at times read a Latin lesson from the holy scriptures to the older students. But one shall not impose such upon him as a duty, but leave it to his own choice, that the youth with particular work in the school be not neglected.

Therefore in order to instruct the children in a Christian way sometime during the week, someone must see to it that such a master is secured who is favorable to and understands the gospel of Christ, and that none other are allowed with the children in this city.

You shall supply one scholarly assistant for the master, also one chorister who shall do a work similar to the other according to the direction of the master, and in addition thereto teach the children to sing. Also there shall be an assistant teacher for the smallest children. To this school will be sent the children of the burghers from the Olden Stadt, Sacke and Altewik.[1]

The other school shall be at St. Catherine's. There you shall maintain one scholarly rector, one chorister, and also one assistant.

To this school shall be sent the children of the burghers from Hagen and Nye Stadt.

With fewer than the seven persons described above you cannot establish the two schools to the best interests of the

[1] These were three of the five precincts of the town.

pupils and authorities. Moreover so long as there are five congregations, it will be impossible to get along with fewer teachers.

. . . .

The children shall attend the choir on the sacred evening and sacred days in that congregation to which their parents belong.

Concerning the Stipends of the Latin Schools

We will diligently endeavor to retain well trained, scholarly assistants in the schools, and not incapable and unintelligent ones. For this reason it is just that we shall not keep them like beggars, but shall pay each one suitably accordingly to his worth, all the while keeping in mind that they need nourishment, clothing, bedding, writing books, and other unexpected necessities which at times cost more than food and drink.

Moreover if a severe illness comes to them that they cannot earn their pay, we will still as our own servants not forsake them in need, since it would be unchristian so long as they can be helped.

And if honest and scholarly assistants happen to come to us who on account of poverty are willing to accept for a time whatever one would offer them, we will nevertheless not seek to take advantage of them so that our ordinance may remain fixed and enduring. If it has no permanency these assistants will run away from it when they can do better and warn others against service with us. For this reason also they willingly become indolent, apathetic, neglectful, and disinclined to work with the children, and illustrate the adage, poor pay, poor work.

. . . .

Therefore it is determined to pay the master at St. Martin a yearly salary of fifty gulden, but in this first year he shall content himself with forty gulden. His assistant shall receive thirty gulden. The chorister also thirty gulden, the fourth assistant twenty gulden.

The rector at St. Catherine's thirty gulden. His assistant twenty and the third twenty gulden.

Such compensation shall be paid quarterly when they will need it.

In addition every youth from the aristocracy and from the rich class shall pay every year eight pennies, and all others four pennies. Furthermore a rich man can send his sons ten years to school for such a sum as he might any year give a servant girl. The others have it even cheaper.

. . . .

For the tuition of such youths shall every schoolmaster take into his class half of the children. The other half shall the assistants divide equally, so that there shall be no discord on account of the children. If the youngest assistant is not as learned as the others, yet he will not have fewer children under his care, and will not be given any lighter task. If they apply diligence with their children, they will perhaps have the more of them.

The schoolmaster shall entrust to one of his assistants the matter of collecting the tuition each half year and give an account of the same.

If some citizens are so unreasonable that they will not pay for their children, let them be remonstrated with in a friendly way. But if there are people so poor, who can pay nothing, and yet would willingly benefit their children, they may go to the managers of the general treasury in their precinct; in such cases they will report such children and bring them to the schoolmaster, according to the will of the Lord, so that in this way instruction and good discipline of the children may become common for both rich and poor.

Moreover when some people during the funeral procession would have the pupils with one of the assistants sing before the coffin German psalms or other sacred songs not to help the dead but to admonish the living, also the Te Deum laudamus or any other song when the bride is led into the church, let the assistants divide the money among themselves. They are not to sing without pay.

We find some burghers among us, who not only gladly pay the tuition for their own children, but also because of special diligence and labor for their children give some assistants free board and other gifts. On such uncertain matters our ordinance can take no action.

 .   .   .   .

Concerning the Dwellings of the Teachers

The two masters shall have fire-places and kitchens, etc.; each one of the assistants a warm room and a bedchamber.

Such dwellings for the schoolmasters and assistants the honorable council will build and maintain to meet the need as heretofore. But if one of the assistants marries and cannot keep house in these quarters, so that there may still be a kitchen and bedchamber, the parish in which he teaches shall provide a dwelling to meet the needs, or procure means from the general treasury.

Concerning the Work in the School

In regard to the work and exercises in the schools, generally it shall be as Philip Melanchthon has described in the book with the title: "Instructions to the visitors in the parishes," etc.

The children shall be divided into three classes, or in three divisions. The first are the smallest, the next the middle-sized, and third the oldest as is stated in the aforementioned book. The first two divisions shall be taught in both schools. The third division, when there is such a division, will be taught only at St. Martin's. Such youth and no other shall the master at St. Martin's accept when the parents desire it, but not without the judgment of the superintendent, who shall examine the youth to see if he is fitted for that third division, so that the rector at St. Catherine's shall not have any offence or that there shall not be any conflict between the two masters.

If the rector at St. Catherine's can and wishes to teach still longer the scholarly youth who have been with him for some time, the parents shall decide to let the youth remain, or which to receive, so that the rector shall not neglect his work on this account in connection with the other two classes.

This third class of the youth will scarcely be formed at first, or rather rarely, and yet it must be begun. Perhaps other assistants and children of burghers, who have formerly been students will attend such or similar lectures which will be delivered before the youth of the third class, as is set forth in the book referred to. This shall be gladly permitted. If they are able to do so, then they may for this service present the master with some food stuffs.

Every diligence and industry in the schools shall serve to the end that the youth be so well exercised in learning Latin that they learn to read well, write correctly, understand the authors which are expounded, speak Latin correctly and constantly write verses and epistles. Furthermore, it will do no harm at certain times to examine and see to it, when they read German, that they do not mix the two languages and read without understanding. That can easily be done when they must explain Latin sentences. It will help the youth over his difficulty to write regularly good Latin epistles. Do not let them learn to speak or read poor Latin if one can do better by them.

These exercises shall continue for such a time until the children are prepared for dialectic and rhetoric, as is described in the aforementioned book.

At the proper time those who have the capacity are likewise to be taught to read Greek and to that end the master shall set forth in Greek the Lord's prayer, or a chapter from the New Testament or something else which is short and easy. In due time they shall learn to decline some words grammatically, yet not too much of this, so that the masters display their learning without benefit to their pupils. To teach Greek before they are well exercised in Latin is for us to lose our entire effort and expense.

In the same way one shall teach them to know and to read the Hebrew letters so as to help in case any of them hereafter enter a higher school where the languages are taught.

. . . .

One shall not burden the children with what they are not able to bear, but keep them diligently employed in learning Latin, as is written in the aforementioned book.

In the same book it is written how at certain times they shall teach God's word and holy scriptures, and shall bring them up in the fear of God and in Christian faith and life, to the honor of God, to the glory of the holy gospel, and for our salvation. Amen.

Concerning the Choristers in the Schools

The two choristers in the two schools shall perform their labors like the other assistants according to the command and will of their respective rectors. Furthermore it is their particular duty to teach all children, large and small, learned and ignorant, to sing (as Philip Melanchthon has stated in the aforementioned book) common songs in German and Latin.

. . . .

Therefore he shall select three or four good boys who can hold the song for him with strong voices, but all the other boys in their parish shall accompany them. Some have poor voices which can be well controlled so that they shall sing low and listen to the others. In this way all children and youth shall learn to sing in the schools.

Concerning the Judgment of the Schoolmasters in Regard to the Youth

When the youth have attended school until they are twelve years old, the schoolmaster shall then announce to the parents in a straightforward way, if any are entirely unable to learn.

The others who can learn readily, he shall, when they are sixteen years old, divide in this manner. When he sees those who though they hitherto have learned well and are sufficiently skilled, but are not so gifted that they can learn still further, these he shall advise that henceforth they shall exercise what they have already learned, and shall take up some honorable and satisfactory vocation. But those who though the smallest of all, are found to be skilled in teaching others and capable in applying their knowledge, let these be dedicated to God that they may serve other people in the spiritual as well as in the temporal affairs of government. Such people are needed. One such is at times better for the public good than ten thousand others.

But that we call here devotion to God—although we should all be dedicated to God—that we do not let these take up manual work; it then becomes very necessary either to send them to other suitable secular employments which have to do with a livelihood, or to send them to study further, so long as they need this, each one to the kind of knowledge to which he is inclined. If they are poor they are to be given help so considerately that they shall be bound to us to serve as our reward when we summon them from the school or from any other service.

We may perhaps find among us also some pious, rich folk who will make special donations to such scholarly and bright poor boys to enable them to study for the best interests of society and the salvation of many people.

We have given our children to become priests and monks. Would it not be better, that we give our children together with our possessions to God, for the benefit and salvation of many people? If they do not become rich in great houses, lands, estates and gold, they will nevertheless be more useful, and God would not abandon them to want.

That the Schools May Be Permanent

The superintendent or highest preacher with his assistant together with five members of the council from the five precincts and the treasurer of the general treasury shall every half-year visit the schools to see if they are being carried on in every particular according to the order first inaugurated. Moreover no winkel [1] schools shall be allowed by which the regular schools may be broken up.

[1] These were private schools by volunteer, wandering teachers.

EARLY PROTESTANT EDUCATORS

Concerning the Elementary German Schools

Two German schoolmasters appointed by the honorable council, shall receive a gift every year from the general treasury. In return they shall be obligated to teach their children at certain times something good from the word of God, the ten commandments, the creed, the Lord's prayer, concerning the two sacraments instituted by Christ, with short explanation and Christian song.

Furthermore the children whom they teach shall give them the reward and pay for their work the more liberally because they do not need to remain at school as long as in the Latin school, and also because these masters have no other compensation.

Concerning the Girls' Schools

Four schools for girls shall be held in four well selected parts of the city, so that the girls are not required to go a great distance from their parents. The honorable council will select and appoint the schoolmistresses, who shall be grounded in the gospel and of good report. Each one shall receive a gift from the general treasury, and shall suffer no need as Christian servants of the entire city. Accordingly they shall bear in mind that they are under obligation to the city to perform such services.

The pay and reward for their labor shall be given by the parents of the girls, so far as they are able, more liberally and abundantly every year, and shall pay the school fees every quarter, and at times what is in the kitchen, because such teaching involves trouble and labor, although it is accomplished in a short time. For the girls need to learn only to read, and to hear some exposition of the ten commandments, the creed and Lord's prayer, and what baptism is and the sacrament of the body and blood of Christ, and to learn to recite some passages from the New Testament concerning the creed, the love and patience on the cross, and some sacred history or story suitable to girls, in order to exercise their memories, moreover in order to impress the gospel of Christ, and in addition to learn Christian song. Such they can learn in a year or at most two years. Therefore let the parents beware that they do not give the schoolmistresses too little for such work even if it takes but a short time to do.

The girls, morever, shall go to school only one or at most two hours per day. The rest of the time they repeat the lesson at home, and also help their parents and learn to keep house, and to observe, etc.

From such girls who have laid hold of God's word there will come useful, skillful, happy, friendly, obedient, God-fearing, not superstitious, and self-willed housewives, who can control their servants, and train their children in obedi-ence and to respect them and to reverence God. And their children will henceforth train their children in the same way, and so on for each generation. But if any evil should happen at any time, we will leave that to God. We should do what God has commanded us. How bad it would be, if we did not further such a good cause for the sake of inexperi-enced youth.

Furthermore if any burgher is very poor, and yet would

gladly have his daughter learn, let him speak to the manager of the general treasury for the poor in his parish, who will attend to the matter for the sake of the Lord.

Concerning Singing and Reading of the School Children in the Churches

Many scholars must confess that it has helped them to learn and to memorize when they were obliged in youth to sing psalms and similar responses. . . .

Therefore we will secure these same benefits to our children, by having them every day, evening and morning, sing and read, which we are pleased to term vespers and mattins. And those who have hitherto learned, shall not begrudge our children; they shall not draw up the bridge when capable people would pass over the water. What has helped them, will help others also, and shall now through God's grace help still more, because the singing shall be controlled and regulated. . . .

The schoolmasters shall see to it that it is not performed otherwise. Moreover now greater diligence shall be applied that the children learn constantly the Latin they sing and read. With this method they will be accustomed to go to the Holy Scriptures as to a play. According every day the same course shall be taken as it is laid down here.

Every work day the chorister at St. Martin's and the chorister at St. Catherine's with all the children of their schools go to the church in the morning at eight, in the evening at two, or at such a time that will not interfere with the services.

SCHOOL ORDINANCES

SCHOOL ORDINANCES

THE laws governing schools in Germany at this time were usually embodied in the "Kirchenordnungen" and were termed *Schulordnungen*. Many of these were issued before the Reformation and several hundred during the sixteenth century.[1] Melanchthon, Luther, and Bugenhagen each wrote a number. Others followed their examples. The free cities of Germany were the first to formulate such school ordinances. These were frequently promulgated by the city councils, or at times by the councils and people together. In the kingdoms and principalities the ruling princes issued the ordinances. Among the first of these were the Saxon Ordinance[2] found under Melanchthon's name, and that of the town of Brunswick under the name of Bugenhagen.[3] The most important was the Grand Ecclesiastical Order of Württemberg issued by Duke Christopher in 1559. This is of greatest significance, for it is the first to make provision for an entire system of schools under state control.

In general, the Hamburg Order of 1529 and the Lübeck Order of 1531 and a number of others followed the model of

[1] For further information concerning these church and school ordinances or orders consult C. L. Robbins, "Teachers in Germany in the Sixteenth Century"; Herzog's "Realencyclopädie für protestantische Theologie," article "Kirchenordnungen."

[2] See p. 180.

[3] See p. 193.

that of Brunswick. Most of these were written by Bugenhagen. Only the provisions for the library, the German writing schools, and the girls' schools are translated and included
here. Because of its importance, more of the elaborate Württemberg school code is included and some topics from the
Pomeranian Order of 1563. After that of Württemberg, the
Saxon school order of 1580 is regarded of highest importance.
It differs but little from that of Württemberg and is, therefore, not included.

SCHOOL ORDINANCE FROM THE HAMBURG CHURCH ORDINANCE [1]
(1529)

Translated by Dr. Albert Henry Newman

Article I

Concerning the Schools [2]

•   •   •   •   •   •   •   •   •   •

Article II

*Concerning the Judgment of the Schoolmaster regarding
the Youth* [3]

•   •   •   •   •   •   •   •   •

[1] VORMBAUM, REINHOLD, "Evangelische Schulordnungen,"
Vol. I, pp. 18–26.
[2] Only the headings of the first four articles are presented
here.
[3] The same as the Brunswick School Ordinance (see above,
p. 193).

SCHOOL ORDINANCES

Article III

That the School May Be Permanent

. . . .

Article IV

Concerning the Lectorium [1]

. . . .

Article V

Of the Library

A library shall be erected not far from the school and the lectorium [see footnote], wherein all books, good and bad, which shall be acquired for this purpose in this city, shall be assembled; they shall be orderly arranged, especially the best, each near others of its kind; keys thereto, one or four, should be in the hands of some, as with the rector and sub-rector and superintendents, that no damage may be done.

Article VI

Of the German Writing-school

It has been thought well that a German school should be held in St. Nicholas School. The masters and two other as-

[1] This was a room where lectures were delivered on the higher subjects such as law, medicine, theology. Such provisions were quite common.

sistants shall have the use of the school free and what belongs to the premises; they also shall have their dwelling for which they shall be obliged to teach their scholars something Christian, also Christian singing. Their remuneration they shall at first receive from their scholars. The commissioners who establish the schools should appoint and pay the writing master, also should see to it that he keep and pay such assistants as in such case are reasonable and needful.

Article VII

Of the Girls' Schools

In every district a girls' school must be held. Such schools, the commissioners of the Council and the deacons of the district shall establish, shall pay the house rent for the chosen school-mistresses out of the general treasury and shall see to it that it has been well spent for the benefit of the girls of the district. For such house-rent shall the school-mistresses be under obligation to have special Christian entertainments having to do with the studies, recitations from the Holy Scriptures, the catechism and Christian songs to be learned, before they receive pay and reward for their work. . . . [The subsequent regulations are taken literally from the Brunswick Church Ordinance.]

SCHOOL ORDINANCES

Translated by Dr. Albert Henry Newman

The most far-reaching step in the organization of Protestant state education took place under Duke Christopher of Württemberg in 1559. His chief motive was to provide pastors and spiritual leaders for his people. To this end he ruled that the endowments of the monasteries should be set apart for religious education in accordance with their original design. His system of schools consisted of three levels "to carry youth from the elements through successive grades to the degree of culture demanded for offices in the church and in the state."

At the bottom were the "particular schools" in the country towns and villages. During the early Middle Ages any school was called a *studium,* and a more pretentious school whose graduates could teach anywhere was called *studium generale.* These "particular" schools were in contradistinction to the old idea of the *generale.* In addition to these small schools, two *pedagogia* were to be established, the one in Stuttgart and the other at Tübingen. These were fully organized schools of five classes leading up to the University. These had boarding departments attached, and provided free living and instruction for a number of boys who intended entering the ministry. Numerous *pedagogia* were es-

[1] VORMBAUM, REINHOLD, "Evangelische Schulordnungen," Vol. I, Part I, pp. 68–71, 102–105, 159–165.

tablished after this model in other principalities and free cities.

In addition to these schools and paralleling their work somewhat were the *cloister* schools. Students entered these at from twelve to fourteen years of age. There were lower and higher cloister schools. These, too, led up to the University. But the higher cloister schools were designed for the training of those students who were not going to the University but were destined for the less important pastorates. At the apex of the system was the University of Tübingen. All these schools taught in the Latin language.

Elementary German schools were allowed for the larger towns only but they are not considered important. Catechical instruction was provided for the villages. Everywhere great effort is to be put forth to discover promising boys and good opportunity provided for their education.

Of the Schools

Inasmuch as upright, wise, learned, skilful and Godfearing men belong to the holy preaching office, to the secular magistracy, administrative offices, and domestic life, and since the schools are the proper means ordained and commanded by God, wherein such people may be educated; as also in the laws the schools and students are endowed and provided with special privileges, and we are reminded to have and maintain the schools and studies; therefore our forefathers appropriated out of their temporal goods a considerable part to monasteries and foundations for the support of schools and studies. Accordingly, that in our principality from their infancy upward, from their elementary studies through the grades, and then still further to the useful languages, seeing that the Old Testament was written in the Hebrew and the New Testament in the Greek language, and that by these studies children may become capable theologians and may be trained in other highly necessary arts, civil government, official duties, and domestic matters; so we ordain, provide and command that in our principality such schools, by our appointed counsellors be established with all industry, and serious attention, and be put into effect without fail. First of all, special care is to be given that in each and every community, whether large or small, the foremost towns as well as the hamlets of our principality, Latin schools with properly qualified teachers be maintained.

And inasmuch as we find that heretofore in our schools a certain amount of diversity as regards teaching, authors and methods of teaching prevailed, which is considered more of a hindrance than a help to the boys, for the good and advantage of the youth we are moved and impelled to establish a uniform school ordinance with distinct division into *Classes, Decurias,* certain authors, hours, recitations and the like, according to which the preceptors are to regulate everything, and shall by no means change anything to suit themselves, so that each school shall accord with every other. And although this ordinance is simply arranged and may have a childish appearance, yet we think that every one who would weigh this work properly will easily appreciate for himself that in matters and affairs pertaining to children one must proceed simply, and that without such childlike beginning greater things are not to be attained.

But inasmuch as this school arrangement with all classes cannot, from lack of teachers and also learners, be entirely and completely put into effect in every one of our schools, and on this account in some localities only the lower classes may be held; neither is it advisable that the young immediately after the first rudiments and before they have been properly trained in grammatical studies and have secured adequate instruction in dialectics and rhetoric, be sent to a University or high-school while so young; also it is not proper for such, in case they are poor, to be admitted to our foundations and bursaries. Accordingly we have caused to be established in our city of Stuttgart for the benefit of the children of our province a special Pedagogium with skilled masters of pedagogy, wherein all classes, and the reading pertaining to the same shall be taught by learned preceptors as may be needed, in order that boys who would be sent to a University before they have studied grammar, dialectics and rhetoric may there continue their studies. In order also that poor indigent boys of good and fruitful talents may be helped and that they may be able to advance through the grades to the highest studies, we purpose that some from the small particular schools who are capable of entering the fifth or at least the fourth class go to the Pedagogium, and to give and extend to them a subsidy or help from our common Church treasury until they are further promoted.

Besides this and in order that as much as possible our poor

country people may be encouraged and helped in educating their children at school, we have also arranged for graded schools in our cloisters (former monasteries) such as the stipend founded at Tübingen some time ago by our benevolent dear lords and fathers of blessed memory, and which we have endowed and fostered still more richly, in order that thereby help may be rendered to our poor rural children who are devoted to study, that thus they may advance grade by grade, and that from the local school the most earnest boys whose parents are unable to help them and who are otherwise qualified according to the Ordinance, shall be admitted into such cloister schools, so that they may proceed therein or in our *Pedagogium* at Stuttgart; to this end we propose to further increase our subsidy and to help them stage by stage to pursue their studies to their completion for their own advancement and welfare and ultimately for the good of the Church of God.

Inasmuch as in our University at Tübingen there are still young boys who are not sufficiently grounded in the precepts of grammar, dialectics and rhetoric to be able to avail themselves fully of the public lectures, we have had established and arranged for their benefit, under the auspices of our University, a Pedagogium, to be provided with capable, learned professors.

As we have in our principality some important and populous hamlets and common hardworking subjects who because of their labor have not all the time needed for teaching and training their children, in order that their laboring children be not neglected in youth, but may be well trained especially in common prayer and catechism and along with these writing and reading, for their own benefit and that of the community, in like manner also trained in singing psalms, and thus may be brought up as Christians, we determine that where heretofore in such hamlets there were sacristies (stations for mass) there be established German schools along with the sacristies, and that counsellors be sent from our organized churches to look after the German schools and sacristies, and that previously examined persons well instructed in writing and reading and capable of instructing the youth in the catechism and in church singing be arranged for.

Everything in the way of Ordinances in regard to such schools as we have in mind follows in an orderly way.

Of Particular Schools

Since now not a little stress is laid upon the youths' being properly guided, instructed and grounded from the beginning of their studies, then following thereupon pursue the more advanced studies on the foundation thus advantageously laid, properly organized schools must be founded and developed in each part of our cities and hamlets, and whereas the youth is hindered as it were at the threshold, unequally or badly instructed and neglected, involving for them very serious difficulty, injury, and hindrances, we hereby command with all earnestness that in all our Principality's Particular Latin Schools the following order, as we have had it compiled and arranged by some who from long experience understand thoroughly these matters, for the instruction and discipline of the boys. Our Church Council deputed for this purpose shall also have authority to appoint and install preceptors and their assistants and to instruct them as to their particular duties, the administration of legal and designated benefices and special privileges through superintendents and our Church Council deputed for this purpose.[1]

* * * * * * * * * *

Of the Cloister Schools

Inasmuch as at present many children of our subjects with good and fruitful minds, because of the poverty of their parents or otherwise have been hindered hitherto in their studies, so that they are not fitted to be held and designated for theology, accordingly we order and will that henceforth only our country children be educated in our cloisters for students and that they be received and admitted as hereafter follows. Accordingly we order and will that henceforth such of our rural children as are qualified for study shall be accepted and admitted into our cloisters on the terms hereinafter set forth.

But inasmuch as cloister institutions such as ours do not have in them young children who require daily care and cleaning, but are established in order that church servants for the teaching and preaching office, so much as ever they

[1] Here follow at length and in much detail regulations as to classes, textbooks, hourly schedule, religious exercises, discipline, examination of teachers, and salaries of the particular schools.

are favored with the blessing of the Almighty, may therein receive the best possible training; to this end also, side by side with other courses, the study of theology, according to the advancement of the students, should be especially pressed. Moreover the parents of young children who attend schools in the hamlets and villages should be on the look-out for boys and students of from twelve to about fourteen years of age, who have good minds and are desirous and capable of higher studies. Furthermore, since it is incumbent upon servants of the church more than others to conduct themselves in an honorable way, but outwardly and in youth so to conduct themselves as they hope to do when older, students in the cloister schools should cultivate side by side with success in studies, a quiet, chaste and self-controlled disposition and behavior.

Likewise those born of Christian, genteel and well-to-do parents should be well educated in a Christian way.

And of the grammar teachers (*Praeceptorum Grammaticae*), according to need and in accord with reports received that in such matters they are in need of no special preceptor or instruction, that they know how to help themselves therein as much as is necessary, and have attained to the fourth class according to our special school arrangement and perhaps to the fifth class, or are ready to be promoted to our Pedagogium at Stuttgart, it is our will that as soon as possible they be promoted to our cloister schools for higher studies, that they may so much the sooner complete the course of their studies and be ready for public service.

But as among them we have found, and graciously consider that some of our subjects are not possessed of sufficient means to keep their children in school long enough to master perfectly the grammatical studies, the question has arisen whether we should allow them to receive help in our Pedagogium; and we have been deterred by the fear lest thereby easily fruitful and capable minds be hindered to the disadvantage of the church, also lest the parents immediately from the beginning might thereby be led so much the less to send their children to school; accordingly we will make the further order, that in some of our schools specially designated for this purpose, the grammatical studies be diligently taught and insisted upon, to the end that those who are not sufficiently practiced in the precepts of grammar, but who have yet reached the third grade (*Classem Tertiam*) in our particular schools, and still more the fourth, and such as might be capable of profiting from the lectures themselves (*lectiones*), may be received; and that then, when they shall have received a promotion (*profectum*), they may be advanced to one of our cloister schools wherein they may pursue the higher arts' studies along with theology and so be graduated.

Moreover for the maintenance of right order and to guard against receiving into our cloister schools faulty, erring or unqualified students, every young man of the class concerned, first of all and before he is admitted to the examination proposed, each candidate must bring with him from his pastor and schoolmaster certificates regarding his scholastic attainments (erudition), talents, and correct conduct and then present them; and then also from our officials of the same locality certificates regarding his age, occupation, demeanor and the temporal means of his parents, and what sort of brothers and sisters he has, and whether these are educated or not, and, if so, to what extent in a Christian way. These testimonials our pastors, schoolmasters, officials, and magistrates (so far as they believe and think that on account of the young man's talents such a subsidy would be well placed upon him, also having ascertained whether his parents, guardians or foster-parents are devout Christians and whether they are willing and anxious for their son to enter the ministry) shall furnish so far as it concerns them. Yet shall they not refer to our Church Council or allow to come before it any young man who is afflicted with a secret or repulsive disease. And as regards these points, in accordance with our emphatic order, no defect, physical, intellectual or educational is to be spoken of before our deputies.

Accordingly that all and each, in order to be received into our cloister schools, after they have presented their satisfactory testimonials shall be examined and tested in our city of Stuttgart, by our head master of the Pedagogium and one of his colleagues, in the presence of two, or at least one, outside of our Church Counsellors, to ascertain whether they are especially qualified for and capable of mastering the studies (*lectiones*) which are to be read and taught in the cloisters; and this with good use and progress without hindrance to themselves or the other students (*auditores*). On the basis of such examination our Counsellors are to report in writing conscientiously and in accord with the facts how they find each candidate, together with their judgment regarding his capabilities.

So now after the candidate has fulfilled all requirements for entrance into some cloister institution, he shall be admitted by our Church Counsellors into a cloister in accordance with his classification (*gradu*) and scholarship wherever a vacancy is found (for this purpose a regular record and catalogue should be in hand, so that at any time they may see from it what sort of boys are in each cloister, and how many vacancies there are). Those thus selected are to be sent at last to our prelates who are required to receive and to support these as others.

No one of our prelates shall admit any young man to our cloister schools without previous examination as aforesaid. However in case there should be a deficiency in the number of students and the prelate should know of a qualified boy, he may advise him to go to our Church Counsellors at Stuttgart with his testimonials as previously mentioned, submit to an examination by the same, and in case he be found fit, he shall then first through these our prelates be admitted.

And while, as set forth at the beginning, the young men all and each who are supported in our cloister schools are under obligations to devote themselves altogether and solely to their studies in order that in time they may be of use to the Church's teaching and preaching service, it is requisite that their parents, guardians, or most closely related friends, obligate themselves thereto in the form hereafter mentioned. . . .

Of German Schools

In order then also that the youth in and about our German schools may be well instructed and trained in the fear of God, right doctrine and good conduct, and that there may be uniformity among them, we would have the following order observed in such matters.

Of Different Kinds of School Children

And inasmuch as in some German schools not only the boys, but also the little girls are sent to school, we determine that in such schools the children be separated, the boys alone and the little girls also be separately placed and taught, and that the schoolmaster by no means allow them to run back and forth among each other, or to have any disorderly relations with each other or to slip together.

Of the Instruction

If then the schoolmaster will teach effectively he should divide them into three groups: The one in which those are placed who are first beginning to learn the alphabet; the second, those who are just beginning to put syllables together. The third, those who are beginning to read and write.

In like manner, under each group special classes are to be formed, so that those of equal aptness to learn in each group may be put together, in order that the children may be stimulated to industry and the work of the schoolmasters may be lessened.

The schoolmasters moreover should not hurry the children overmuch or promote them until each one has well and properly learned in the order arranged for.

Also special pains should be taken that they learn the letters rightly from the start. To this end the order of the alphabet should be occasionally broken up and with the letters mixed up the child should be asked to name some of the letters indiscriminately.

In like manner he should exercise them with letters of similar form, questioning them as to the names of the letters and requiring them to point them out to him in the alphabet.

And thereupon, when they have first learned to name the letters correctly in every way, they shall be taught to pronounce clearly the syllables, and at last to pronounce the words syllable by syllable, indiscriminately and intelligently. They shall be taught not to mumble the last syllables.

Then when the child can read tolerably well, it shall be instructed in writing; and the writing copies shall be made in a special book which the child should have for this purpose, and he should diligently apply himself to making good German letters.

And then see to it that the children have also for their writing special booklets, and that these be carefully examined for them, having regard to defects in the form of the letters, the joining and adjustment thereof and the like, that each child be kindly spoken to in a low tone and shown in a friendly way how each defect should be corrected, in the meantime the teacher guiding his hand in making such corrections.

And meanwhile the children before all things shall be brought to the fear of God. Some would hereby direct that the schoolmasters do not allow any child to make use in their learning of any scandalous, shameful, sectarian books or any other kind of useless fictitious writings, in order that they may learn in Christian booklets, such as the volume in which are the Catechism, the Book of Psalms, the Proverbs of Solomon, Jesus Sirach, the New Testament, and the like.

But especially it is our opinion that the Catechism, as it is embraced in our Church Order, that thus uniformity may be preserved, be drilled into the children, or that they become familiar with it, so that they will memorize it, practice it, and rightly understand and comprehend it. To this end the schoolmasters should set apart one particular day each week and one particular hour of the same day, and thus practice and exercise with them; also give them simple instruction therein and explain it to them in a way that they can understand.

Also the children in the school, pair by pair, boys against boys, girls against girls, shall compete in asking and answering questions about the Catechism, and in recitation of its contents, in order that they may become accustomed to do the same publicly before the church at the time of the Catechism.

In like manner the boys on certain days and at certain

hours every week shall become accustomed to church singing, instructed and practiced therein.

And on some days in the week, as may be convenient, they
shall be given one piece after the other from the German
Ciston (musical term) and they shall be instructed therein.

. . . .

On the German Writing and Reckoning Scholars

Inasmuch as there is no small need of good public scribes
and accountants in our country, states and city clerical offices,
and moreover for the advantage of ourselves and the com-
monweal good home management will be of no little importance.

Accordingly we ordain and will that by our official counsellors three pious, religiously zealous German schoolmasters, who are good draughtsmen and scribes, also can calculate with the pen and upon the lines, apt to teach, and
diligent, should be commissioned; namely, the one to go to
Stuttgart, another to Tübingen, and the other to Brach.
In these places they shall establish their schools in good
order which shall be assigned and given to them for this
purpose. And in order that so much the better qualified
men of the sort may be brought here and retained we would
grant them, outside of the common church fund, a yearly
subsidy besides the regular school-salary, and also that hous-
ing be provided and maintained in these cities.

School Ordinance from the Pomeranian Church Ordinance, 1563 [1]

. . . .

On Schools for Young Women

In the large cities schools for young women shall be maintained and the Council with the pastor shall appoint God-fearing, honorable persons to teach them to read and write.

These schoolmasters or schoolmistresses shall be provided with free furnished dwelling and besides have from the pupils a tuition fee and fuel-money. In case the public funds permit, the visitors may allow a salary in addition or may entrust this office to one or two preachers.

The young women shall go to school four hours every week-day; the rest of the time they shall learn housekeeping with their parents. Before all things they shall be diligently instructed in the Catechism, in psalms, Christian songs, and proverbs from the Holy Scriptures; they shall also be required to attend prayer and preaching.

Of German Writing Schools

All hedge schools shall be forbidden and not tolerated, nor shall it be permitted to everyone to set up as a public scribe. But German scribes shall be appointed by the Council and paid from the public treasury. If they be pious and not antagonistic to the pastor they may be given a gratuity from the treasury; but they receive their pay from their scholars;

[1] *Ibid.,* pp. 177–178.

they should teach them to read, to write correctly and well, and to cipher, and shall hold them to the Catechism and to the sermons, as a form shall be presented to them regarding these things with the advice of the pastor.

But should the council and the pastors unite and arrange the German school with the Latin, the scribe shall be subordinated to the ordinary rector of the school, his German pupils on Sundays he shall let go to the church choir, also shall not admit boys without the judgment of the pastor and the schoolmaster in order that the school property may not be damaged.

About Libraries

The old useful books should be brought together in the cities and kept safely in a library. The deacon of the treasury shall, as much as possible, increase the library every year, especially with German Bibles and volumes of Luther's works. The parish clergy shall pray and exhort the people to increase the libraries through legacies. The pastor and deacons shall see to it that an inventory is made and the library assiduously guarded.

The Young Women's Cloister

Much stress is laid upon the training of the young women as well as the boys during the early years in a knowledge of God and in all virtues, so that those also who may fail of an opportunity to marry may end their life in blessed chastity and honorableness and may always be found in a Christian standing and walk. Therefore Christian law requires that some cloisters be left for the young women for their education and maintenances.

But what sort of a rule or order is to be made or enacted, according to which the aforesaid young women are to be controlled and related, a common delegation of landowners in cooperation with us, the provincial princes, after mature deliberation has preceded will submissively determine in proper time.

JOHN CALVIN

LIFE AND WORK

THOUGH not so broad as Luther in educational interests and sympathies, Calvin was more profound; though he did not write nearly so much, his influence was as penetrating and as widely spread. He was the son of the secretary to the Bishop of Noyon, in France, where he saw the light of day in 1509. His father intended to make him a priest and to this end provided him every educational advantage. Needless to say, Calvin was a precocious lad. At fourteen he was off to Paris to attend the *Collège de la Marche* where Mathurin Cordier, an excellent scholar, became his teacher and lifelong friend. Soon he was ready to go forward and transferred to the famous *Collège de Montaigu*. By some peculiarity of fate, several years after Calvin left, the celebrated founder of the Jesuit order, Ignatius Loyola, sat on the same benches and under the same masters.

Calvin's father came under the displeasure of the church and as a consequence advised him to turn his attention to the study of law. To this end he went to the universities of Orleans and Bruges. His heart, however, was not in the legal profession, though no one would accuse him of lacking a legalistic mind. But it was rather the classical languages and literatures which now captured his interest. When twenty-two years of age his father died, and he felt free to pursue his own course. He thereupon returned to Paris. About this time, rather suddenly it appears, he broke with the Catholic Church and became strongly evangelical. Three years later he wrote the first edition of the "Institutes of the Christian Religion," which marked him as one of the few profound theologians of the day. In 1536 he settled as pastor in Geneva but two years later was compelled to leave. He spent three years in Strassburg, which was a liberal city and the refuge for religious exiles. Here he acted as pastor of the church for French Protestant refugees and lectured on theology in the local college. In close articulation with the college a classical gymnasium had just been founded by the celebrated humanist, John Sturm. As this school became the model for secondary education for much of central Europe, we can well believe it influenced the plans of Calvin.

The year 1541 found Calvin recalled to Geneva where he was step by step to build up "the Rome of Protestantism" and to exert a dominant influence in France, eastern Germany, Holland, England, and Scotland. He died in 1564.

From his return to Geneva, Calvin held steadily in view the establishment of a school. Due to numerous difficulties he was unable to realize his full plans until 1559 when he reorganized the existing schools into the college and academy. This was a Latin school and a theological seminary combined and under the strict and immediate supervision of the church authorities, though supported by the city. It was conducted with military rigor and with all the conviction of a religious zealot.

Calvin showed no particular interest in elementary vernacular education. He complained to the council of Geneva that there were too many small schools, and the number was reduced to four, one for each quarter of the city. A small fee was charged in these schools. He required that only those boys should be allowed to attend these elementary schools who could not learn Latin. Even then in the interest of uniformity, he demanded that all the pupils in these schools should be assembled every Wednesday at the great college so that there might be some religious instruction in common. The teachers of the elementary schools were required to be examined and supervised.

One can get an adequate conception of Calvin's educational program only by holding steadily in view his theory of government and Christian life. His genius was realized in welding church, state, and home into one combined institution for the purpose of the instruction, discipline, training, and control of the entire body of people. In the home the parents taught the children the catechism and Christian living. This work was strictly supervised by the elders and *consistorium*. Homes were visited every year to see that these regulations were carried out. The church was used for instruction in orthodox religious doctrines and living and for instruction in the catechism for old and young. The college and academy had the same end in view but naturally combined rigorous classical training with the religious instruction. This Calvinistic view of education can readily be seen in the educational arrangements of the Huguenots, the Dutch Reformed, the Puritans, and the Scotch Presbyterians.

VIEW OF HUMAN NATURE

Education has always been profoundly affected by the view held of the goodness or evil of human nature. Some look upon infants as pure and good and their childish play and conduct as innocent of wrongdoing and worthy of encouragement. Others, again, regard human nature as fundamentally sinful and absolutely incapable of any good act or thought. Calvin was one of the most extreme of this line of thinkers. He believed in the total depravity of man, that is to say, that all elements of man are positively evil and depraved, his flesh, sensuous appetites, affections, will, and intellect. His statement of original sin is given here.

Translated by John Allen [1]

Original sin, therefore, appears to be an hereditary pravity and corruption of our nature, diffused through all the parts of the soul, rendering us obnoxious to the Divine wrath, and producing in us those works which the Scripture calls "works of the flesh." And this is indeed what Paul frequently denominates *sin*. The works which proceed thence, such as adulteries, fornications, thefts, hatreds, murders, revellings, he calls in the same manner "fruits of sin"; although they are also called "sins" in many passages of Scripture, and even by himself. These two things therefore should be distinctly observed: first, that our nature being

[1] ALLEN, JOHN, "Institutes of the Christian Religion by John Calvin," Vol. I, pp. 229–231.

so totally vitiated and depraved, we are, on account of this very corruption, considered as convicted and justly condemned in the sight of God, to whom nothing is acceptable but righteousness, innocence, and purity. And this liableness to punishment arises not from the delinquency of another; for when it is said that the sin of Adam renders us obnoxious to the Divine judgment, it is not to be understood as if we, though innocent, were undeservedly loaded with the guilt of his sin; but, because we are all subject to a curse, in consequence of his transgression, he is therefore said to have involved us in guilt. Nevertheless we derive from him, not only the punishment, but also the pollution to which the punishment is justly due. Wherefore Augustine, though he frequently calls it the sin of another, the more clearly to indicate its transmission to us by propagation, yet, at the same time, also asserts it properly to belong to every individual. And the Apostle himself expressly declares, that "death has therefore passed upon all men, for that all have sinned"; that is, have been involved in original sin, and defiled with its blemishes. And therefore infants themselves, as they bring their condemnation into the world with them, are rendered obnoxious to punishment by their own sinfulness, not by the sinfulness of another. For though they have not yet produced the fruits of their iniquity, yet they have the seed of it within them; even their whole nature is as it were a seed of sin, and therefore cannot but be odious and abominable to God. Whence it follows, that it is properly accounted sin in the sight of God, because there could be no guilt without crime. The other thing to be remarked is, that this depravity never ceases in us, but is perpetually producing new fruits, those works of the flesh, which we have before described, like the emission of flame and sparks from a heated furnace, or like the streams of water from a never failing spring. Wherefore those who have defined original sin as a privation of the original righteousness, which we ought to possess, though they comprise the whole of the subject, yet have not used language sufficiently expressive of its operation and influence. For our nature is not only destitute of all good, but is so fertile in all evils that it cannot remain inactive. Those who have called it *concupiscence* have used an expression not improper, if it were only added, which is far from being conceded by most persons, that every thing in man, the understanding and will, the soul and body, is polluted and engrossed by this concupiscence; or, to express it more briefly, that man is of himself nothing else but concupiscence.

Wherefore I have asserted that sin has possessed all the powers of the soul, since Adam departed from the fountain of righteousness. For man has not only been ensnared by the inferior appetites, but abominable impiety has seized the very citadel of his mind, and pride has penetrated into the inmost recesses of his heart; so that it is weak and foolish to restrict the corruption which has proceeded thence, to what are called the sensual affections, or to call it an incentive which allures, excites, and attracts to sin, only what they style the sensual part. In this the grossest ignorance has been discovered by Peter Lombard, who, when investigating the seat of it, says that it is in the flesh, according to the testimony of Paul, not indeed exclusively, but because it principally appears in the flesh; as though Paul designated only a part of the soul, and not the whole of our nature, which is opposed to supernatural grace. Now, Paul removes every doubt by informing us that the corruption resides not in one part only, but that there is nothing pure and uncontaminated by its mortal infection. For, when arguing respecting corrupt nature, he not only condemns the inordinate motions of the appetites, but principally insists on the blindness of the mind, and the depravity of the heart; and the third chapter of his Epistle to the Romans is nothing but a description of original sin. This appears more evident from our renovation. For "the Spirit," which is opposed to "the old man" and the "flesh," not only denotes the grace, which corrects the inferior or sensual part of the soul, but comprehends a complete reformation of all its powers. And therefore Paul not only enjoins us to mortify our sensual appetites, but exhorts us to be renewed in the spirit of our mind; and in another place he directs us to be transformed by the renewing of our mind. Whence it follows, that that part, which principally displays the excellence and dignity of the soul, is not only wounded but so corrupted, that it requires not merely to be healed, but to receive a new nature. How far sin occupies both the mind and the heart, we shall presently see. My intention here was only to hint, in a brief way, that man is so totally overwhelmed, as with a deluge, that no part is free from sin; and therefore that whatever proceeds from him is accounted sin; as Paul says that all the affections or thoughts of the flesh are enmity against God, and therefore death.

THE AUTHORITY OF SCRIPTURE MUST NOT BE SUBJECTED TO THE INTERPRETATION OF HUMAN REASON

Translated by John Allen [1]

This, then must be considered as a fixed principle, that, in order to enjoy the light of true religion, we ought to begin with the doctrine of heaven; and that no man can have the least knowledge of true and sound doctrine, without having been a disciple of the Scripture. Hence originates all true wisdom, when we embrace with reverence the testimony which God hath been pleased therein to deliver concerning himself. For obedience is the source, not only of an absolutely perfect and complete faith, but of all right knowledge of God. And truly in this instance God hath, in his providence, particularly consulted the true interests of mankind in all ages.

.　.　.　.　.　.　.　.　.　.　.

Since we are not favored with daily oracles from heaven, and since it is only in the Scriptures that the Lord hath been pleased to preserve his truth in perpetual remembrance, it obtains the same complete credit and authority with be-

[1] ALLEN, JOHN, "Institutes of the Christian Religion by John Calvin," Vol. I, pp. 73, 75, 78, 79–80.

lievers, when they are satisfied of its divine origin, as if they heard the very words pronounced by God himself.

.   .   .   .

The principal proof, therefore, of the Scriptures is every where derived from the character of the Divine Speaker. The prophets and apostles boast not of their own genius, or any of those talents which conciliate the faith of the hearers; nor do they insist on arguments for reason; but bring forward the sacred name of God, to compel the submission of the whole world.

.   .   .   .

Religion appearing, to profane men, to consist wholly in opinion, in order that they may not believe anything on foolish or slight grounds, they wish and expect it to be proved by rational arguments, that Moses and the prophets spoke by divine inspiration. But I reply, that the testimony of the Spirit is superior to all reason. For, as God alone is a sufficient witness of himself in his own word, so also the word will never gain credit in the hearts of men, till it be confirmed by the internal testimony of the Spirit. It is necessary, therefore, that the same Spirit, who spake by the mouths of the prophets, should penetrate into our hearts, to convince us that they faithfully delivered the oracles which were divinely intrusted to them. And this connection is very suitably expressed in these words: "My Spirit that is upon thee, and my word which I have put in thy mouth, shall not depart out of thy mouth, nor out of the mouth of thy seed, nor out of the mouth of thy seed's seed, forever." . . .

Let it be considered, then, as an undeniable truth, that they who have been inwardly taught by the Spirit, feel an entire acquiescence in the Scripture, and that it is self-authenticated, carrying with it its own evidence, and ought not to be made the subject of demonstration and arguments from reason; but it obtains the credit which it deserves with us by the testimony of the Spirit.

DOCTRINE OF CIVIL GOVERNMENT

Influenced chiefly by the Old Testament, Calvin viewed the church and the state as a theocracy. The two have the same origin and derive their authority from the same exalted source, the Creator. Furthermore, both serve the same ultimate end, the realization of the divine will in the world. Two organs, one organism—that is the readiest formula by which to explain their relation. They differ in function, but by harmony of operation they realize an identical purpose. They are equally concerned with the regulation of the life, conduct, and thinking of the individual men and women who compose the community. Home, church, and state form a cooperative institution for the discipline, regimen, and instruction of all their members. Schools are but one of the agencies in the carrying out of this complete system of surveillance, supervision, guidance, and instruction. Calvin's theory of the functions of the state are to be seen in the extracts below. The supervision, which Calvin instituted, of the home by the church-state was the most unique feature of his system of training.

JOHN CALVIN

On Civil Government

Translated by John Allen [1]

Civil government is designed, as long as we live in this world, to cherish and support the external worship of God, to preserve the pure doctrine of religion, to defend the constitution of the Church, to regulate our lives in a manner requisite for the society of men, to form our manners to civil justice, to promote our concord with each other, and to establish general peace and tranquillity. . . .

It is equally as necessary to mankind as bread and water, light and air, and far more excellent. For it not only tends to secure the accommodations arising from all these things, that men may breathe, eat, drink, and be sustained in life, though it comprehends all these things while it causes them to live together, yet, I say, this is not its only tendency; its objects also are, that idolatry, sacrileges against the name of God, blasphemies against his truth, and other offences against religion, may not openly appear and be disseminated among the people; that the public tranquillity may not be disturbed; that every person may enjoy his property without molestation; that men may transact their business together without fraud or injustice; that integrity and modesty may be cultivated among them; in short, that there may be a public form of religion among Christians, and that humanity may be maintained among men. Nor let any one think it strange that I now refer to human polity the charge of the due

[1] ALLEN, JOHN, "Institutes of the Christian Religion by John Calvin," Vol. II, pp. 634–635, 641.

243

maintenance of religion, which I may appear to have placed beyond the jurisdiction of men. For I do not allow men to make laws respecting religion and the worship of God now, any more than I did before; though I approve of civil government, which provides that the true religion which is contained in the law of God, be not violated, and polluted by public blasphemies, with impunity. . . .

Therefore, as religion holds the first place among all the philosophers, and as this has always been regarded by the universal consent of all nations, Christian princes and magistrates ought to be ashamed of their indolence, if they do not make it the object of their most serious care. We have already shown that this duty is particularly enjoined upon them by God; for it is reasonable that they should employ their utmost efforts in asserting and defending the honour of him, whose vicegerents they are, and by whose favour they govern. And the principal commendations given in the Scripture to the good kings are for having restored the worship of God when it had been corrupted or abolished, or for having devoted their attention to religion, that it might flourish in purity and safety under their reigns. On the contrary, the sacred history represents it as one of the evils arising from anarchy, or a want of good government, that when "there was no king in Israel, every man did that which was right in his own eyes." These things evince the folly of those who would wish magistrates to neglect all thoughts of God, and to confine themselves entirely to the administration of justice among men; as though God appointed governors in his name to decide secular controversies, and disregard that which is of far greater importance—the pure worship of himself according to the rule of his law. But a rage for universal innovation, and a desire to escape with impunity, instigate men of turbulent spirits to wish that all the avengers of violated piety were removed out of the world.

Divine Origin of State

Translated by Henry Beveridge [1]

I confess that God would have the world to be governed by laws and polity, so that reins should not be wanting to curb the unbridled movements of men, and that for that purpose he has established kingdoms, princedoms, and dominations, whatever relates to civil jurisdiction; of which things he wills to be regarded as the Author; that not only should their authority be submitted to for his sake, but we should also revere and honour rulers as the vicegerents of God and ministers appointed by him to discharge a legitimate and sacred function. And therefore I also acknowledge that it is right to obey their laws and statutes, pay tribute and taxes, and other things of the same nature; in short, bear the yoke of subjection ultroneously and willingly; with the exception, however, that the authority of God, the Sovereign Prince, must always remain entire and unimpaired.

[1] CALVIN, JOHN, "Tracts Containing Treatises on the Sacraments, Catechism of the Church of Geneva, Forms of Prayer, and Confessions of Faith," translated by Henry Beveridge, Vol. II, p. 135.

Catechism of the Church of Geneva Being a Form of Instruction for Children in the Doctrine of Christ

Translated by Henry Beveridge [1]

Like Luther some few years earlier, Calvin wrote a catechism for the instruction of children. It was first published in French in 1536 and in Latin two years later. This original publication was subjected to a radical revision both in form and content by Calvin himself and republished in 1541. A comparison with Luther's catechism is instructive. Calvin treats five topics in about fifty-eight pages: faith, the Commandments, prayer, the Word of God, and the Sacraments. Only a page or two can be given here as a sample of his method of treatment.

Dedication

John Calvin to the Faithful Ministers of Christ Throughout East Friesland, Who Preach the Pure Doctrine of the Gospel. . . . What shall our feelings be concerning posterity, about which I am so anxious, that I scarcely dare to think? Unless God miraculously send help from heaven, I cannot avoid seeing that the world is threatened with the ex-

---

[1] CALVIN, JOHN, "Tracts Containing Treatises on the Sacraments, Catechism of the Church of Geneva, Forms of Prayer, and Confessions of Faith," translated by Henry Beveridge, Vol. II, pp. 35, 37–39.

tremity of barbarism. I wish our children may not shortly
feel, that this has been rather a true prophecy than a conjec-
ture. The more, therefore, must we labour to gather together, by our writings, whatever remains of the Church
shall continue, or even emerge, after our death. Writings of
a different class will show what were our views on all subjects in religion, but the agreement which our churches had
in doctrine cannot be seen with clearer evidence than from
catechisms. For therein will appear, not only what one man
or other once taught, but with what rudiments learned and
unlearned alike amongst us, were constantly imbued from
childhood, all the faithful holding them as their formal sym-
bol of Christian communion. This was indeed my principal
reason for publishing this Catechism.

. . . .

To the Reader

It has ever been the practice of the Church, and one carefully attended to, to see that children should be duly instructed in the Christian religion. That this might be done
more conveniently, not only were schools opened in old
time, and individuals enjoined properly to teach their families, but it was a received public custom and practice, to
question children in the churches on each of the heads, which
should be common and well known to all Christians. To
secure this being done in order, there was written out a
formula, which was called a Catechism or Institute. There-
after the devil miserably rending the Church of God, and

bringing upon it fearful ruin, (of which the marks are still too visible in the greater part of the world,) overthrew this sacred policy, and left nothing behind but certain trifles, which only beget superstition, without any fruit of edification. Of this description is that confirmation, as they call it, full of gesticulations which, worse than ridiculous, are fitted only for apes, and have no foundation to rest upon. What we now bring forward, therefore, is nothing else than the use of things which from ancient times were observed by Christians, and the true worshippers of God, and which never were laid aside until the Church was wholly corrupted.

Catechism of the Church of Geneva
Of Faith

Master.—What is the chief end of human life?

Scholar.—To know God by whom men were created.

M.—What reason have you for saying so?

S.—Because he created us and placed us in this world to be glorified in us. And it is indeed right that our life, of which himself is the beginning, should be devoted to his glory.

M.—What is the highest good of men?

S.—The very same thing.

M.—Why do you hold that to be the highest good?

S.—Because without it our condition is worse than that of the brutes.

M.—Hence, then, we clearly see that nothing worse can happen to a man than not to live to God.

S.—It is so.

M.—What is the true and right knowledge of God?

S.—When he is so known that due honour is paid to him.

M.—What is the method of honouring him duly?

S.—To place our whole confidence in him; to study to serve him during our whole life by obeying his will; to call upon him in all our necessities, seeking salvation and every good thing that can be desired in him; lastly, to acknowledge him both with heart and lips, as the sole Author of all blessings.

M.—To consider these points in their order, and explain them more fully—What is the first head in this division of yours?

S.—To place our whole confidence in God.

M.—How shall we do so?

S.—When we know him to be Almighty and perfectly good.

M.—Is this enough?

S.—Far from it.

M.—Wherefore?

S.—Because we are unworthy that he should exert his power in helping us, and show how good he is by saving us.

M.—What more then is needful?

S.—That each of us should set it down in his mind that God loves him, and is willing to be a Father, and the author of salvation to him.

M.—But whence will this appear?

S.—From his word, in which he explains his mercy to us in Christ, and testifies of his love towards us.

M.—Then the foundation and beginning of confidence in God is to know him in Christ?

S.—Entirely so.

M.—I should now wish you to tell me in a few words, what the sum of this knowledge is?

S.—It is contained in the Confession of Faith, or rather formula of Confession, which all Christians have in common. It is commonly called the Apostle's Creed, because from the beginning of the Church it was ever received among all the pious, and because it either fell from the lips of the Apostles, or was faithfully gathered out of their writings.

M.—Repeat it.

S.—I believe in God the Father Almighty, maker of heaven and earth; and in Jesus Christ, his only Son, our Lord, who was conceived by the Holy Ghost, born of the Virgin Mary, suffered under Pontius Pilate, was crucified, dead, and buried: he descended into hell; the third day he arose again from the dead; he ascended into heaven, and sitteth on the right hand of God the Father Almighty, from thence he shall come to judge the quick and the dead. I believe in the Holy Ghost: the holy Catholick Church; the communion of saints; the forgiveness of sins; the resurrection of the body; and the life everlasting. Amen.

Supervision by the Elders [1]

"The office of the elders," say the ordinances,[2] "consists in having surveillance over the life of every individual."

[1] Kampschulte, F. W., "Johann Calvin, Seine Kirche und Sein Staat in Genf," Vol. I, pp. 436–437.

[2] These ordinances were passed by the city council at the insistence of Calvin.

They are first of all the appointed overseers of the congregation and must especially watch over and examine carefully the entire life within and without the Church, in general and in particular. Nothing must escape their attention. It is clear, the oath of office has already provided for this—that they pay heed, first and foremost to the orthodoxy of the members of the congregation. Contradiction of the recognized teachers of the Church is the initial error to which their official instruction directs their attention. And not merely the spoken word, but also the attitude and intention are to be observed. Furthermore, the elders shall seek to discover experimentally whether the believer follows conscientiously in other respects the commandments of the Church, whether he attends preaching frequently, not merely on Sundays, whether he receives the sacrament regularly and reverently, teaches his children constantly as a Christian should do, and sends them to school. Finally they have also to oversee the moral conduct of the individual. This shall be done with great diligence and care. The home of every citizen, the most prominent as well as the least, stands open at all times for the members of the consistorium [1] in order that they may be able to make a visitation when it is considered advisable. To make such visitation they have not merely a right, but from the right arises the duty. At least once a year, states an amendment to the ordinances, shall every residence in the city be visited, in order to gain information through questions, examinations, observations,

[1] A governing body of the church appointed to supervise and direct the conduct of its members.

in regard to the religious training and moral behaviour of the individual families and members of families. "Plenty of time shall be taken so as to make the investigation thoroughly." Two members of the college, a minister and a layman shall take charge of a precinct, and the representative of this precinct must accompany them and introduce them into the individual families "so that no one may escape the examination." Most important of all is the daily and noiselessly exercised control. To render it easier and thus more effective it was expressly prescribed, so to control the election to the consistorium that in every precinct a lay elder should be chosen, who "can have his eye everywhere."

BY-LAWS OF THE ACADEMY OF GENEVA [1]

Translated by Ernestine F. Leon

These laws are presented to English readers for the first time. To appreciate their significance it is necessary to compare them with the three-class Latin school of Melanchthon some thirty years earlier, the contemporary plan of Sturm at Strassburg, and the Ratio Studiorum of the Jesuits. The institution at Geneva was divided into two parts, the gymnasium which served as a classical, preparatory school for boys and the academy which was in effect a seminary for theological study. It formed the model for Calvinistic institutions in many places, among them the universities of

[1] BORGEAUD, CHARLES, "Histoire de l'Université de Genève," pp. 626–635, Geneva, 1900.

Leyden and Edinburgh, and was thought to have influenced the establishment of Emmanuel College, Cambridge University, in which so many of the founders of Harvard received their training. If the more obvious aspects of Emmanuel do not suggest the Academy of Geneva, at least a strong kinship of spirit is unmistakably present. As a matter of fact, Calvin's educational views, which emphasized the unification of humanism and religious instruction to a greater extent than other contemporary educators, traveled hand in hand with the triumph of his doctrines.

The By-laws of Calvin's school were printed in 1559 by the firm of Robert Estienne (Stephanus) in Latin and in the vernacular. By order of the authorities, the French text was appended to the church ordinances published in 1561. (New editions in 1562, 1568, 1569.) In 1576 the board approved the revised edition. There was a new French edition in 1578, a Latin translation in 1593, and again a "Regulation for Schools" in 1609.

The remarks of Theodore Beza, which serve as preface to the By-laws of the Academy in the pamphlet of Estienne, end with the following summary:

"If anyone follows the By-laws of the Academy correctly, there are in all, each week, twenty-seven lectures in the curriculum of the public school (i. e. the university proper), to wit, three in theology, eight in Hebrew, in the Greek, three in ethics, five in orators or poets, three in physics or mathematics, five in dialectic or rhetoric. But in a private school, which is divided into seven classes (i. e. the preparatory department or gymnasium) there are seventy classes each week, aside from reviews. But if (as we hope, relying on the goodness of God) God who was the author of those plans will also further them, thought shall be taken not alone for the completion of the program which has been initiated but also for the addition of the other subjects i. e. for the teaching of jurisprudence and medicine."

Concerning the Faculty of the Gymnasium

Teachers suitable to instruct in the individual classes are to be chosen with good and clear conscience by a board of ministers and professors. When chosen, they are to be presented to the honorable senate and the appointment confirmed in accord with its opinion.

They shall be on hand promptly in their class-rooms and not omit prescribed lessons without just cause. If some adequate reason does compel them to miss classes, they shall promptly advise the principal to make provision for the students. This shall be done either by securing a substitute or by temporarily combining two related classes into one.

While teaching, the instructors shall observe decorum both in dress and in manner. They shall offer no adverse criticism of the authors whom they are to interpret but faithfully explain their meaning. If any passage seems to be excessively obscure, or displaced, or carelessly written, they shall respectfully call it to the attention of their hearers. They shall keep the boys in order, scold the impudent and lazy and punish them in proportion to their faults. They shall teach especially the love of God and hatred of vice. They are not to leave the class-room unless the lesson is finished, (as far as that is possible). But when the signal is given, each should immediately dismiss his class, in the order which we shall describe.

They shall cultivate a mutual and truly Christian harmony among themselves. They shall in no way criticize each other while teaching. If any disagreement arises, they shall refer it to the rector of the university and argue their sides as Christian gentlemen. If he cannot reconcile the disagreement immediately, let him refer it to the board of ministers who shall interpose their authority.

Concerning the Principal

The principal shall be chosen and appointed, just as we have said. He shall be a man of proven piety, of at least fair scholarship, and especially, above all, a man endowed with a gentle disposition and of a character completely free from harshness, that he may be a model to all the students by the example of his life and patiently fulfill his office, in spite of the annoyances involved therein.

It shall be his duty, besides the ordinary supervision of his school, to look into the character and perseverance of his colleagues, to spur on the slow, to remind all of their duty, to preside at all public castigations in the assembly-room, and finally to see that the bell is sounded at the proper time, whenever necessary and that the individual class-rooms appear clean and tidy.

It shall not be right for the assistant teachers to make any innovation without consulting him. He shall report on all happenings to the rector.

Concerning the Students of the Gymnasium

The principal and his assistant teachers shall divide all the students of a private school (i. e. the preparatory school or gymnasium) into four sections not according to classes but according to the districts of the city. They shall note each section in their rolls and give this roll to four assistant teachers. Then each group of students shall be assigned to its own building in accord with its district.

In the individual halls, in accord with the ruling of the honorable senate, a place shall be assigned for scholars from the proper district and it shall be illegal for any others to use it.

The individual scholars, on Wednesday mornings and on Sundays, both in the morning and at the time for catechism and also afternoon assembly shall all gather promptly in their own halls and sitting in their own places shall listen to the discussions reverently and attentively.

In each hall, some one of the assistant teachers shall be present on time. He shall carefully observe his own students. When the assembly is over, when it shall prove necessary, he shall order the roll to be called. He shall make note of both the absent and the inattentive. Then the following day, those who have been at fault, shall be publicly punished in school in proportion to their misdeeds.

On Monday, Tuesday, Thursday and Friday, in summer at six a. m., in winter at seven, the students shall meet, each in his own class-room.

In each class, they shall be divided into groups of ten. The groups of ten shall be formed in accord with their proficiency, without regard to social rank or age. The proctors shall take their seats first in their own groups of ten and shall carefully oversee these.

When they assemble, they shall begin in their class-rooms with the special prayers of the catechism and each shall in turn reverently recite these prayers on his own day.

Afterward the roll shall be called. If anyone is absent or tardy, after the reason is given, he shall either be excused or punished mildly. Lying, in such cases, shall be punished especially.

Then they shall, in summer, listen to the teacher for one and a half hours. After that there is recess of half an hour for breakfast, without any confusion and with prayers preceding. Then in summer, instruction shall go on until nine. But in winter, they shall be taught from seven until nine, in such a way that breakfast does not hinder the recitation. It shall be taken while the boys are reciting the assigned text. When the morning assignments are over, let the Lord's prayer be recited with a short offering of thanks, in every class by each in turn. As they leave, they shall be given their assignment. And finally, all shall be accompanied home according to custom by two of the assistant teachers of lowest rank, namely of the seventh, sixth, fifth and fourth classes in turn.

On the same days, returning from dinner to school at eleven, both in winter and summer, they shall reverently sing psalms until noon. They shall receive instruction from noon till one. Then an hour shall be devoted partly to a lunch, partly to writing or other studies. From two to four, they shall be instructed. When four o'clock sounds, all shall meet in the assembly hall. Then if any noteworthy public occurrence is to be brought to their attention, it is to be commented on with fitting dignity in the presence of the principal and teachers of the classes, with a moral drawn in accord with the crime. Afterwards, three persons shall daily recite in turn, the Lord's prayer, the confession of faith and the ten commandments in French with careful attention, and finally, as they go home, let proper respect be paid the principal.

On Wednesday mornings (as has been stated) let them hear a religious sermon. After dinner from eleven till twelve, let them be distributed in tens to the individual classes and debate with restraint. Then recreation shall be allowed till three o'clock, but in such a way that all silly sport be avoided. From three to four, twice each month, the students shall hold declamations before an assembly of the entire school. On the two remaining Wednesdays, some theme shall be proposed on which all the boys shall practice their written style. This theme shall be corrected the next day. The lower classes shall do some other task according to the judgment of the teachers. Then they shall be dismissed, in the manner described above.

On Saturday mornings, the lessons of the entire week shall be reviewed. After dinner, from eleven to twelve, as has been said, they shall debate. Then recess from lessons shall be given till three. From three to four the boys (except in two classes, the first and second, which we shall discuss individually) shall recite the part of the catechism to be explained the next day and shall be taught informally in accord with their capacity. Afterward, as we have said, they are to be dismissed.

They shall spend all Sunday in hearing religious worship and in meditating on sermons.

The week before Holy Week (Maundy Thursday), one of the ministers shall give a short sermon on the Lord's supper in the assembly room and exhort all to harmony and piety.

SPECIAL RULES FOR CLASS SEVEN

Here the pupils shall be taught to recognize the letters of the alphabet, then to form syllables from the Latin-French alphabet, then to read French fluently and finally Latin also, from the Latin-French catechism. If age permits, here the boys shall learn to write.

RULES FOR CLASS SIX

In this class, the first and simplest elements of declension and conjugation shall be given in the first six months. In the remaining six months, there shall be given a thorough elementary explanation of the parts of speech and of their properties so that the pupils may compare French with Latin and in addition practice simple exercises in Latin. Here also the boys shall be improved in writing and become accustomed to using Latin.

RULES FOR CLASS FIVE

In this class, a more exact explanation of the parts of speech and the more elementary rules of syntax shall be given. The "Bucolics" of Vergil shall be offered. Some practice in style begins here.

RULES FOR CLASS FOUR

In this class, the rules for Latin syntax shall be completed. The shorter and more intimate letters of Cicero shall be offered. Short easy subjects shall be assigned for themes in imitation of the style of these letters.

The pupils shall have explained to them the quantities of syllables, embraced in a few rules, with reading from Ovid's "Elegies," "De Tristibus" ("Tristia") and "De Ponto" ("Epistulae ex Ponto").

Finally, the boys shall be taught in the simplest possible manner the reading, declension, and conjugation of Greek.

RULES FOR CLASS THREE

Here Greek grammar shall be taught with more detail, so that the boys may closely observe the rules of both lan-

JOHN CALVIN

guages, (i. e. Latin and Greek) and practice composition in them alternately. From among the authors, these especially are to be read: Cicero's "Letters," "De Amicitia," "De Senectute" in Greek and Latin, Vergil's "Aeneid," Caesar's "Commentaries," Isocrates' parenetic orations (the hortatory orations, two to Nicocles and one to Demonicus) as circumstances admit.

RULES FOR CLASS TWO

Here history shall be taught, in Latin from Livy, in Greek from Xenophon, Polybius, or Herodian. Of the poets, Homer shall be read by each in turn. The elements of dialectic, i. e. the divisions of propositions and the figures of argumentation (nothing more) shall be explained. They shall be taught as thoroughly as possible propositions and arguments from the writers who are studied, and especially from Cicero's "Paradoxa" and his shorter orations but without any attention to the technique of oratory.

On Saturdays, from three to four, the Greek Gospels shall be read to them directly.

RULES FOR THE FIRST CLASS

In this class, finally there shall be added to the rudiments of dialectic which have alone been taught, the five voices, categories, places, and proofs, but from some scholarly manual. They shall add the elements of rhetoric and especially those which pertain to stylistic expression.

The use of the individual rules shall be carefully and thoroughly shown in the more artistic speeches of Cicero and also in the "Olynthiacs" and "Philippics" of Demosthenes, likewise in Homer and Vergil, in such a way that the bare propositions may be carefully sorted out, then their adornments explained and compared with the rules themselves.

They are to practice style carefully. They are to have two declamations a month, as we have said, on Wednesdays.

Saturdays from three to four, let them hear read some one of the letters of the apostles.

Concerning the Rector of the School

The rector of the school, a man of conspicuous piety and learning shall be chosen in the fear of and reverence for God, on the first of May, from the board of ministers and professors, by the general vote of this board. When chosen, he shall be presented to the honorable senate and his election confirmed by its authority.

He shall attend to the administration of the entire institution. Negligent professors and teachers, even the principal, are to be reminded by him of their duty. If disagreements arise among students, he shall settle them either by the weight of his own influence, or if it becomes necessary, by resorting to the authority of the ministers.

All students who are to attend the lectures of public professors, shall come to consult with him and be advised by him to present themselves first of all to the honorable senate and according to custom, receive from it the right of domicile. After this, they shall then subscribe in their own writing to the confession of faith (in the form in which we shall append it to these by-laws) and be recorded on the roll of the students.

Likewise he shall give a testimonial of character and attainments, after carefully making inquiry, to such students as ask it.

He shall never call a meeting of the students beyond those stated, unless the senate has given him permission.

He shall fill his office for two years. Then either another man shall be chosen or the same re-elected.

Concerning Vacations

In the autumn, there shall be a vacation for all classes of the entire school for three weeks. On the first Friday of every month, the public professors shall be given vacation from afternoon lectures (except public theological disputations).

Concerning Promotions

Each year, three weeks before the first of May, a public theme in French shall be proposed in the assembly hall at noon by some one of the public professors in turn. The individual students in each class shall take this down according to their own degree of proficiency.

Then the pupils of each class, changing rooms, at sight, without recourse to books, without outside aid, shall by themselves translate the assigned theme into Latin within five hours.

And that there may be no dishonesty, the teacher of the second class shall supervise the pupils of the first class, the teacher of the first the second, etc. Those in charge shall maintain a careful supervision and conduct the examination in all fairness.

When the themes have been collected and arranged in order in groups of ten, the individual teachers shall bring them without any tampering to the principal.

The next and following days, up to the first of May, the rector with the aid of the public professors shall examine the exercises of the individual classes in order. After the corrections are indicated, and the boys called in, in groups of ten and questioned in the presence of their teacher, the class to which each is to be promoted shall be decided in accord with the opinion of the examiners.

On May first, (unless it happens to fall on a Sunday, in which case the ceremony shall be postponed to the next day) the entire school shall assemble in St. Peter's church. If it seems advisable to the honorable senate, there shall be present some one of the syndics or senators, together with the ministers of the Gospel and the professors, the principal and the assistant teachers. In this assembly, the rector of the school shall read these by-laws aloud and recommend them in a short speech. Then from each class, the two pupils who have shown themselves superior to the rest in application and scholarship shall receive at the hand of the syndic or senator who is present some small prize which may seem

appropriate to the honorable senate and they shall respectfully express their thanks. Then after the rector has made
a short commendatory address, students of the first or second
class shall with proper modesty read some original composition in either prose or verse, if available. Finally after the
rector has given the benediction and prayers have been recited, the gathering shall be dismissed.

That day shall be a holiday for the entire school.

If any student seems to his teachers to have made so much
progress that he can be promoted to a higher class before the
end of the year, the teacher shall mention him to the principal, who shall make written record of all students of this
type. Then on the first of October, the rector shall meet with
the teachers in the gymnasium and make a decision in
regard to the matter. But if at some other time of the year,
any student seems fit to be promoted out of order, he shall
be promoted out of order, with the full consent of the rector.

Concerning Public Professors

Three public professors, namely for Hebrew, Greek, and
the liberal arts shall be chosen and confirmed in the manner
specified for the others.

They shall teach two hours a day on Mondays, Tuesdays,
and Thursdays, one on Wednesday and Friday afternoons
and be free from lecturing on Saturdays. Sundays shall be
devoted to attending religious services.

On Fridays they shall attend a convocation which they

themselves summon and a council of the ministers whenever this is possible.

The professor of Hebrew shall in the morning immediately after services expound some book of the Old Testament with the rabbinical commentaries. After lunch, in winter from twelve to one, in summer from one to two, he shall lecture on Hebrew grammar.

The professor of Greek, following the professor of Hebrew in the morning, shall discuss some work on ethical philosophy from Aristotle or Plato or Plutarch, or some Christian philosopher. Then after lunch in winter from one to two, in summer from three to four, he shall lecture in turn on some one of the more moral Greek poets, orators or historians.

The professor of liberal arts shall in the morning for half an hour following the professor of Greek, lecture on a physical problem.

After lunch in winter from three to four, in summer from four to five, he shall carefully expound Aristotle's "Rhetoric," Cicero's more famous orations or "De Oratore."

The two professors of theology, shall lecture on the Scriptures on Mondays, Tuesdays, and Wednesdays, each in turn on alternate weeks from two to three in the afternoon.

Concerning Public Scholars

Public scholars, as has been said before, shall give their names to the rector, subscribe to the confession of faith, and conduct themselves with piety and decorum.

Those who wish to train in theology shall be recorded on a separate roll and each in turn on Saturdays from two till three shall publicly expound some scriptural passage, some one of the ministers in turn directing the entire procedure. Then they shall hear the criticism of the minister who is in charge. In this criticism it shall be proper for any of those present to give an opinion but with proper reverence in the fear of God.

These students shall likewise each month write on what are known as the fixed points of doctrine, neither in a spirit of idle curiosity nor with sophistication, nor embracing false doctrine. They shall consult early in their course with the professor of theology. Then they shall defend these points publicly against those who offer opposing arguments. Opportunity for discussion shall be given to any one. All sophistry, all curiosity, all sacrilegious boldness in corrupting the word of God, all evil contention and obstinacy shall be ruled out. All shall be discussed pro and con in a spirit of reverence and holiness. The theologian who is in charge of the disputation shall guide all discussion by his wisdom and explain difficult questions in accord with the word of God.

Here follows the formula of the "Confession of Faith" to which all public scholars were bound to subscribe before the rector. It is a fairly detailed statement of Calvin's theological doctrine with special emphasis on opposition to what he considered heresy. Several prominent men of the time who are known to have studied at Geneva do not have their names appearing on the records, probably because of their refusal to sub-scribe to this "Confession of Faith." Since the require-ment had a tendency to discourage students from regis-tering at Geneva, it was abolished officially in 1576. In 1584, the academic oath was substituted. Students sub-scribing to this merely promised to live properly and to support the laws of the republic of Geneva and of the school.

Formula of the Oath Which the Rector Is Bound to Give to the Illustrious Senate

I promise and swear that I (by the grace of God) will faithfully perform my duty in this office to which I am called: that is carefully to inspect the condition of the en-tire school so that all difficulties which arise may be properly adjusted in accord with the rules laid down for the scholars.

Likewise that I will encourage all proposed students of the public school to hold themselves in obedience and re-spect to our lords and not to tolerate immoral or licentious students. But if any do not wish to return to the right path by gentle warning, I will report them to the authorities, that the latter may attend to this delinquency.

Likewise I will see to it in so far as I am able that the students live peacefully, honorably and with decorum.

JOHN CALVIN

Formula of the Oath Which Teachers of the Public and Private Schools Are Bound to Take

I promise and swear that I will faithfully conduct myself in the office entrusted to me: that is, in good faith and conscience I will strive that the boys and other students be well instructed.

I will give the lectures assigned to me by our noble authorities and within my province will see to it that the school is governed in the best possible way and bring it about as far as I am able (by the grace of God) that the students live peacefully, honorably, and with decorum so that their lives may be in accord with the glory of God and the peace and tranquillity of the commonwealth.

JOHN KNOX

LIFE AND WORK

JOHN KNOX was another of the remarkable group of religious reformers who helped to re-lay the foundations of education in the sixteenth century. The sphere of his greatest influence was primarily his native Scotland. Through Scotch Presbyterianism, however, his influence was felt in England and more profoundly still in America. The effects of his educational leadership upon our country have never been sufficiently evaluated.

Knox was born in 1505 and received a good education in a grammar school and later at St. Andrews University. On his conversion he left the Catholic priesthood and became a Protestant minister in England. During the persecutions under Queen Mary he found it necessary to flee to the continent where he remained for some five years. During a lengthy sojourn in Germany he came into contact with Lutheranism, and later, while living in Geneva, he espoused the views of Calvin. His educational contribution is found especially in the "Book of Discipline" which though never adopted by the Scottish parliament had profound influence on the reestablishments of schools. His views of education in some ways lean more toward those of Luther, though his theology and principles of government are thoroughly Calvinistic. Knox passed away in 1572.

Order of Schools [1]

(1556)

We are not ignorante that the Scriptures make mention of a fourthe kynde of Ministers left to the Churche of Christe, which also are very profitable, where tyme and place dothe permit. But for lacke of opportunitie, in this oure dispersion and exile,[2] we can not well have the use thereof; and wolde to God it were not neglected where better occasion serveth.

These Ministers are called Teachers or Doctors, whose office is to instructe and teache the faithfull in sownde doctrine, providing with all diligence that the puritie of the Gospell be not corrupt, either through ignorance, or evill opinions. Notwithstandyng, considering the present state of thynges, we comprehend under this title suche meanes as God hathe in his Churche, that it shuld not be left desolate, nor yet his doctrine decaye for defaut of ministers thereof.

Therefore to terme it by a worde more usuall in these our days, we may call it th'Order of Schooles, wherein the highest degree, and moste annexed to the ministerie and governement of the Churche, is the exposition of Godes Worde, which is contayned in the Olde and Newe Testamentes.

But becawse menne cannot so well proffet in that knowledge, except they be first instructed in the tonges and humaine sciences, (for now God worketh not commonlie by

[1] "The Form of Prayers and Ministration of the Sacraments," etc., read in the English Congregation at Geneva, 1556, David Laing, "The Works of John Knox," Vol. IV, p. 177.

[2] Written while Knox was in exile in Geneva.

miracles,) it is necessarie that seed be sowen for the tyme to
come, to the intent that the Churche be not left barren and
waste to our posteritie; and that Scholes also be erected,
and Colledges mayntayned, with juste and sufficient sti-
pendes, wherein youthe may be trayned in the knowledge
and feare of God, that in their ripe age they may prove
worthy members of our Lorde Jesus Christ, whether it be
to rule in Civill policie, or to serve in the Spirituall ministerie, or els to lyve in godly reverence and subjection.

THE BOOK OF DISCIPLINE

The plan for the reformation of the church in Scotland was set forth in the first "Book of Discipline"
which was written by John Knox and five other ministers associated with him. It was introduced into the
Scottish parliament in 1560, but the lords and nobles
declined to sanction it. As will be seen, provision was
made in it for schools which were to be financed by the
accumulated wealth of the church and monasteries,
now being overthrown. The nobility were unwilling
to vote for this method of disposing of the great riches
of the churches and monastic institutions; for they
hoped to divide the spoils of these disintegrating estab-
lishments among themselves. Even though it was never
legally adopted, the scheme of education in the "Book
of Discipline" is notable nevertheless, as it proposes a
national system of schools according to the Calvinistic principles under state and church control. Comparison should be made with the "School Ordinance"

of Württemberg, just a year earlier. Provision is made for family instruction, church instruction, parish schools, grammar schools, and universities. Supervision is provided for in each case. From the time of the great Celtic missionary movement in the eighth and ninth centuries the Scotch people had retained an unusual devotion to education. The Reformation built the new institutions upon this interest which had so long been active.

The Preface to The Buke of Discipline [1]

To the Great Counsall of Scotland now admitted to (the) Regiment, by the Providence of God, and by the commoun consent of the Estaittis Thairof, Your Honouris Humble Servitouris and Ministeris of Christ Jesus within the same, wishe Grace, Mercy, and Peace from God the Father of Oure Lord Jesus Christ, with the Perpetuall encrease of the Holye Spirite.

FOR THE SCHOLLIS

Seeing that the office and dewtie [2] of the godlie Magistrat is nocht onlie [3] to purge the Churche of God from all superstitioun, and to set it at libertie from bondage of tyrranis; but also to provide, to the uttermost of his power,

---

[1] "The Works of John Knox," collected and edited by David Laing, Vol. II, pp. 208–221.

[2] Duty.

[3] Not only.

how it may abide in the same puritie to the posteriteis following; we cannot but frelie communicat our judgementis with your Honouris in this behalf.

1. The Necessitie of Schollis

Seing that God hath determined that his Churche heir [1] in earth, shall be tawght not be angellis but by men; and seing that men ar born ignorant of all godlynes; and seing, also, now God ceassith to illuminat men miraculuslie, suddanlie changeing thame, as that he did his Apostlis and utheris in the Primitive Churche: off necessitie it is that your Honouris be most cairfull for the virtuous educatioun, and godlie upbringing of the youth of this Realme, yf eathir ye now thirst unfeanedlie [2] (for) the advancement of Christis glorie, or yit desire the continewance of his benefits to the generatioun following. For as the youth must succeed till us, so aucht we to be cairfull that thei have the knawledge and eruditioun, to proffit and confort that whiche aucht to be most deare to us, to wit, the Churche and Spouse of the Lord Jesus.

Off necessitie thairfore we judge it, that everie severall Churche have a Scholmaister appointed, suche a one as is able, at least, to teache Grammer and the Latine toung, yf the Toun be of any reputatioun. Yf it be Upaland,[3] whaire the people convene to doctrine bot once in the weeke, then

[1] Here.
[2] Unfeignedly.
[3] Upon-land: living in the country, rather than the town.

must eathir the Reidar [1] or the Minister thair appointed, take cayre over the children and youth of the parische, to instruct them in thair first rudimentis, and especiallie in the Catechisme,[2] as we have it now translaited in the Booke of our Common Ordour, callit the Ordour of Geneva. And farther, we think it expedient, that in everie notable toun, and especiallie in the toun of the Superintendent, (there) be erected a Colledge, in whiche the Artis, at least Logick and Rethorick, togidder with the Tongues, be read by sufficient Maisteris, for whome honest stipendis must be appointed: as also provisioun for those that be poore, and be nocht able by them selfis, nor by thair freindis, to be sustened at letteris, especiallie suche as come frome Landwart.[3]

The frute and commoditie heirof shall suddanlie appeare. For, first, the youtheid and tender children sall be nurischit and brocht up in virtue, in presence of thair freindis; by whose good attendence many inconvenientis may be avoided, in the which the youth commonlie fallis, eathir by too muche libertie, whiche thei have in strange and unknawin placis, whill thei can not rule them selfis; or ellis for lacke of gude attendence, and of suche necessiteis as thair tender aige requireth. Secoundarlie, The exercise of the children in everie Churche shall be great instruction to the aigeit.[4]

[1] A lector who was appointed to read the Scriptures publicly in the churches.

[2] See pp. 246–250 for Calvin's catechism. It was translated and printed at Edinburgh in 1564.

[3] Inland.

[4] Aged.

Last, The great Schollis callit Universiteis, shall be re-
pleanischit with those that be apt to learnyng; for this must
be cairfullie provideit, that no fader, of what estait or con-
ditioun that ever he be, use his children at his awin fantasie,
especiallie in thair youth-heade; but all must be compelled
to bring up thair children in learnyng and virtue.

The riche and potent may not be permitted to suffer thair
children to spend thair youth in vane idilnes, as heirtofore
thei have done. But thei must be exhorted, and by the censure
of the Churche compelled to dedicat thair sones, by good
exercise, to the proffit of the Churche and to the Common-
wealth; and that thei must do of thair awin expensses, becaus thei ar able. The children of the poore must be supported
and sustenit on the charge of the Churche, till tryell be
tackin, whethir the spirit of docilitie be fund in them or
not. Yf thei be fund apt to letteris and learnyng, then may
thei not (we meane, neathir the sonis of the riche, nor yit
the sonis of the poore,) be permittit to reject learnyng; but
must be chargeit to continew thair studie, sa that the
Commoun-wealthe may have some confort by them. And
for this purpose must discreit, learned, and grave men be
appointit to visit all Schollis for the tryell of thair exercise,
proffit, and continewance; to wit, the Ministeris and Elderis,
with the best learned in everie toun, shall everie quarter tak
examinatioun how the youth hath proffitted.

A certane tyme must be appointed to Reiding, and to
learning of the Catechisme; ane certane tyme to the Grammar, and to the Latine toung; ane certane tyme to the Artis,

Philosophie, and to the (other) Toungis; and a certane to that studie in which thei intend cheaflie to travell [1] for the proffit of the Commoun-wealth. Whiche tyme being expired, we meane in everie course, the children must eathir proceid to farther knawledge, or ellis thei must be send to sum handie-craft, or to sum othir proffitable exercise; provideit alwayis, that first thei have the forme of knawledge of Christiane religioun, to wit, the knawledge of Goddis law and commandimentis; the use and office of the same; the cheaf articulis of our beleve; the richt forme to pray unto God; the nomber, use, and effect of the sacramentis; the trew knawledge of Christ Jesus, of his office and natures, and suche otheris, as without the knawledge wheirof, neathir deservith (any) man to be named a Christiane, neather aught ony to be admittit to the participatioun of the Lordis Tabill: [2] And thairfore, these principallis aught and must be learned in the youth-heid.

II. The Tymes Appointed to Everie Course

Two yearis we think more then sufficient to learne to read perfitelie,[3] to answer to the Catechisme, and to have some entresse in the first rudimentis of Grammar; to the full accomplischement whairof, (we meane of the Grammar,) we think other thre or foure yearis at most, sufficient. To the Artis, to wit, Logick and Rethorick, and to the Greik toung,

[1] To labor at.
[2] The Lord's supper.
[3] Perfectly.

foure yeiris; and the rest, till the aige of twenty-foure yearis
to be spent in that studye, whairin the learnar wald proffit
the Churche or Commoun-wealth, be it in the Lawis, or
Physick or Divinitie: Whiche tyme of twenty-foure yearis
being spent in the schollis, the learnar most be removed to
serve the Churche or Commoun-wealth, unless he be fund
a necessarie Reidare in the same Colledge or Universitie.
Yf God shall move your heartis to establische and execut
this Ordour, and put these thingis in practise, your hole
Realme, (we doubt nott,) within few yearis, shall serve the
self of trew preacharis, and of uther officiaris necessarie for
your Common-wealth.

III. The Erectioun of Universiteis

The Grammar Schollis and of the Toungis being erectit
as we have said, nixt we think it necessarie thair be three
Universities in this whole Realme, establischeit in the Tòunis
accustumed. The first in Sanctandrois,[1] the secound in
Glasgow, and the thrid in Abirdene.

And in the first Universitie and principall, whiche is
SANCTANDROIS,[1] thair be thre Colledgeis. And in the first Colledge, quhilk is the entre of the Universitie,[2] thair be four
classes or saigeis:[3] the first, to the new Suppostis,[4] shalbe
onlie Dialectique; the nixt, onlie Mathematique; the thrid

[1] The University of St. Andrews.
[2] Which is the entrance of the university.
[3] Forms.
[4] A member of the university.

of Phisick onlie; the fourt of Medicine. And in the secound Colledge, twa classes or seigeis: the first, in Morall Philosophie; the secound in the Lawis. And in the thrid College, twa classes or seigeis: the first, in the Toungis, to wit, Greek and Hebreu; the second, in Divinitie.

IV. Off Reidaris, and of the Greis, off Tyme, and Studye [1]

Item, In the first College, and in the first classe, shallbe ane Reidar of Dealectique, wha shall accomplische his course thairof in one yeare. In the Mathematique, whiche is the secound classe, shalbe ane Reidar who shall compleit his course of Arithmetique, Geometrie, Cosmographie, and Astrologie, in ane yeare. In the third classe, shalbe ane Reidar of Naturall Philosophie, who shall compleit his course in a yeare. And wha efter thir thre yearis,[2] by tryell and examinatioun, shall be fund sufficientlie instructit in thir aforesaid sciences, shall be Laureat and Graduat in Philosophie. In the fourt classe, shall be ane Reidar of Medicine, who shall compleit his course in five years: after the study of the whiche tyme, being by examinatioun fund sufficient, thei shall be graduat in Medicine.

Item, In the Secound Colledge, in the first classe, one Reader onlie in the Ethicques, Œconomicques, and Politiques, who shall compleit his course in the space of one yeare. In the secound classe, shall be tuo Reidaris in the Municipall and Romane Lawis, who sall compleit thair

[1] Of readers and of degrees and time of study.
[2] And who after their three years.

coursses in four yeares; after the whiche tyme, being by examination fund [1] sufficient, thei shalbe graduat in the Lawis.

Item, In the third College, in the first classe, ane Reidar of the Hebreu, and ane uther of the Greek toung, wha sall compleit the grammeris thairof in half ane yeare, and the remanent of the yeare, the Reidar of the Hebreu shall interpreit ane booke of Moses, the Propheitis, or the Psalmes; sa that his course and classe shall continew any yeare. The Reidar of the Greek shall interpreit some booke of Plato, togidder with some place of the New Testament. And in the secound classe, shalbe tuo Reideris in Divinitie, that ane in the New Testament, that uthir in the Auld, who sall compleit thair course in five yearis. After whiche tyme, who sall be fund by examinatioun sufficient shall be graduat in Divinitie.

Item, We think expedient that nane [2] be admittit unto the first Colledge, and to be Suppostis of the Universitie, onles he have frome the Maister of the Schole, and the Minister of the toun whair he was instructed in the toungis, ane testimoniall of his learnyng, docilitie, aige, and parentage; and likewayis triall to be tane [3] be certan Examinatouris, deput be the Rectour and Principallis of the same, and yf he be fund sufficientlie instructit in Dialectick, he shall incontinent, [4] that same yeare, be promoted to the classe of Mathematicque.

[1] Found.
[2] No one.
[3] Taken by certain examiners, deputized by the rector.
[4] Immediately.

Item, That nane be admittit to the classe of the Medicine bot he that shall have his testimoniall of his tyme weall spent in Dialecticque, Mathematique, and Phisicque, and of his docilitie in the last.

Item, That nane be admittit unto the classe of the Lawis, but he that shall have sufficient testimoniallis of his tyme weill spent in Dialecticque, Mathematique, Phisique, Ethick, Œconomiques, and Pollitiques, and of his docilitie in the last.

Item, That nane be admittit unto the classe and seige of Divines bot he that shall have sufficient testimonialles of his tyme weill spent in Dialecticque, Mathematicque, Phisique, Ethique, Œconomique, Morall Philosophie, and the Hebreu toung, and of his docilitie in the Morall Philosophie and the Hebru toung. But neathir shall suche as will applye them to hear the Lawis, be compelled to heir Medicine; neathir suche as applye them to hear Divinitie be compellit to hear eathir Medicine or yit the Lawis.

Item, In the Secound Universitie, whiche is *GLASGU,* shalbe twa Colledgeis alanerlie.[1] In the first shalbe ane classe of Dialecticque, ane uther in Mathematicque, the thrid in Phisique, ordourit in all sortis as Sanctandrois.

Item, In the Secound Colledge, four classes; the first in Morall Philosophie, Ethiques, Œconomiques, and Pollitiques; the secound of the Municipale and Romane Lawis; the thrid of the Hebreu toung; the fourt in Divinitie: Which shall be ordourit in all sortis, conforme to it we have writtin in the ordour of the Universitie of Sanctandrois.

[1] Only.

284

The Thrid Universitie of ABIRDENE shall be conforme to this Universitie of Glasgou, in all sortis.

Item, We think neidfull, that thair be chosin of the body of the Universitie to everie Colledge a man of learnyng, discretioun, and diligence, who shall resave the haill rentis [1] of the Colledge, and distribute the same according to the erectioun of the Colledge, and shall dalie hearkin the dyet comptis; [2] adjoynyng to him oulklie [3] ane of the Readeris or Regentis, above whome he shall (take) attendance upoun thair diligence, alsweill [4] in thair reading, as exercitioun of the youth in the mater taught; upoun the polecye and uphold [5] of the place; and for punischement of crymes, shall hald ane oulklie conventioun [6] with the haill memberis of the Colledge. He shall be comptabile [7] yearlie to the Superintendent, Rectour, and rest of the Principallis convened, about the first of November. His electioun shalbe in this sort: Thair shalbe thre of the maist sufficient men of the Universitie, (not Principallis alreaddie,) nominat by the memberis of the College, sworne to follow thair conscience, whais Principall is departed, and publictlie proponed throu the whole Universitie. Efter the whiche tyme eght dayis, the Superintendent by him self or his speciall Procuratour, with the Rectour and rest of the Principallis, as ane chap-

---

[1] Receive the whole rentals.
[2] Shall daily keep an account of the board.
[3] Uniting with himself weekly one, etc.
[4] As well in their reading as exercise, etc.
[5] Upon the administration and support.
[6] A weekly assembly.
[7] Accountable.

tour convened, shall conferme ane of the three thei think maist sufficient, being afore sworne to do the same with singill ee, but respect to feid [1] or favour.

Item, In everie Colledge, we think neidfull at the least ane Steward, ane Cooke, ane Gardnar, ane Portar, wha shall be subject to discipline of the Principale, as the rest.

Item, That everie Universitie have ane Beddale subject to serve at all tymes throuchout the whole Universitie, as the Rectour and Principallis shall command.

Item, That everie Universitie have ane Rectour chosin from yeare to yeare as shall follow. The Principallis being convened with the haill [2] Regentis chaptourlie, shall be sworne, that everie man in his roume shall nominat suche one as his conscience shall testifie to be maist sufficient to beare suche charge and dignitie; and thre of them that shalbe oftest nominat shalbe put in edict publictlie, fiftene dayis afore Michaelmess; and then shall on Michaelmess Evin convene the hoill [3] Principallis, Regentis, and Suppostis that ar graduat, or at the least studyit thair tyme in Ethiques, Œconomiques, and Pollitiques, and na utheris youngare; and everie natioun, [4] first protestand [5] in Goddis presence to follow the sinceir ditement [6] of thair consciences, shall nominat ane of the saie [7] thre; and he that hes monyest votis shall

[1] Without regard to enmity.
[2] Whole body of professors.
[3] When all the members are present.
[4] A body of students.
[5] Avowing.
[6] Dictates.
[7] Said.

be confermit be the Superintendent and Principall, and his dewitie with ane exhortatioun proponed unto him: And this to be the 28 day of September; and thairefter aithis to be takin *hinc inde,* off his just and godlie governement, and of the remanentis lauchfull submissioun and obedience. He shall be propyned [1] to the Universitie at his entre, with ane new garment, bearing *Insignia Magistratus;* and be halden monethlie [2] to visie everie Colledge, and with his presence decore [3] and examyn the lectionis and exercitioun thairof. His assessoris shalbe ane laweir and ane theolog,[4] with whois advise he shall decide all questionis civill, betwix the memberis of the Universitie. Yf ony without the Universitie persew ane member thairof, or be persewit be ane member of the samin, he shall assist the Provest and Baillies in thei casses, or uthir judgeis competent, to see justice be ministred. In likewise, yf ony of the Universitie be criminallie persewit, he shall assist the Judgeis competent, and se that justice be ministered.

Item, We think it expedient, that in everie Colledge in everie Universitie, thair be twenty-four bursaris,[5] divided equalie in all the classes and seigeis, as is above exprimit: that is, in Sanctandrois, seventie-tua bursaris; in Glasgou, fourtye-eyght bursaris; in Abirdene, fourty-eyght; to be sustened onlie in meit upon the chargeis of the Colledge; and be admitted at the examinatioun of the Ministerie and

[1] Presented.
[2] Be required monthly.
[3] Adorn and examine the lectures.
[4] Assistants shall be a lawyer and theologian.
[5] An endowment given to a student.

chaptour of Principallis in the Universitie, alsweill in docilitie of the personis offerit, as of the habillitie [1] of thair
parentis to sustene thame thair selvis, and nocht to burding
the Common-wealth with thame.

V. Off Stipendis and Expensses Necessarie

Item, We think expedient, that the Universiteis be doted [2]
with temporall landis, with rentis and revenewis of the
Bischopriks temporalitie, and of the Kirkis Collegiat, sa far
as thair ordinarie chargeis shall require; and thairfore, that
it wald please your Honouris, be advise of your Honouris
Counsall and voit [3] of Parliament, to do the samin. And to
the effect the same may be schortlie expediat, we have recol-
lected the soumes we think necessarie for the samin.

.   .   .   .

Item, We have thocht gude for building and uphald of
the placis, ane general collect be maid; and that everie Erlis
sone,[4] at his entre to the Universitie, shall gif fourtye schillingis, and sicklike at everie graduatioun, 40 schillingis.
Item, Everie Lordis sone sicklike at ilk [5] tyme, 30 schillingis;
ilk fre halding [6] Baronis sone, twentye schillingis: everie
Fewar and substantious Gentilmannis sone, ane mark. *Item,*
Everie substantious Husband and Burges sone, at ilk tyme,

[1] Ability.
[2] Endowed.
[3] Vote.
[4] Son of an earl.
[5] Same.
[6] Free-holding.

ten schillingis: *Item,* Everie ane of the rest, (excepting the Bursaris,) 5 schillingis at ilk tyme.

And that this be gathered in ane commoun box, put in keiping to the Principall of the Theologeanes, everie Principall havand ane key thairof, to be comptit ilk yeare [1] anis, with the relictis [2] of the Principallis to be layed into the samin, about the fivetene day of November, in presence of the Superintendent, Rectour, and the hoill Principallis; and, at thair hoill consent, or at the least the most part thairof, reservit and employit onlie upoun the building and uphalding of the placis, and repairing of the same, as ever necessitie shall require. And thairfore, the Rectour with his assistance shall be haldin to visite the placis ilk yeir anis, incontinent efter he be promoted, upoun the last of October, or thairby.

VI. Off the Privilege of the Universitie

Seing we desire that Innocencie shall defend us rather than Privelege, we think that ilk persoun of the Universitie shuld answeir before the Provest and Baillies of ilk town whaire the Universities ar, of all crymes whairof thai ar accusit, onlie that the Rectour be Assesour to thame in the saidis actionis. In civill materis yf the questioun be betwix memberis of the Universitie on ilk side, making thair residence and exercitioun thairin for the tyme, in that case the partie callit shall not be haldin to answer, but onlie before

[1] Counted once each year.
[2] Residue.

the Rectour and his Assesouris heirtofore expremit. In all uthir casses of civill persute, the generall reule of the Law to be observit, *Actor sequatur forum rei, &c.*

Item, That the Rectour and all inferiour memberis of the Universitie be exempted frome all taxationis, impostis, chargeis of weir, or ony otheir charge that may onerat or abstract [1] him or thame from the cair of thair office; suche as Tutorie, Curatorie, Deaconrie, or ony siclike, that ar establischeit, or heirefter shall be established in our Commonwealth; to the effect, that but trubill,[2] that ane may wait upoun the upbringing of the youth in learnyng, that othir bestow his tyme onlie in that most necessarie exercitioune.

All othir thingis tuiching the bookes to be red in ilk classe, and all suche particular effaries,[3] we refer to the discretioun of the Maisteris, Principallis, and Regentis, with thair weill advisit Counsallis; not doubting but yf God sall grant quietnes, and gif your Wisdomes grace to set fordward letteris in the sort prescribed, ye shall leave wisdome and learnyng to your posteritie, ane treasure more to be estemed nor ony [4] earthlie treasure ye ar abill to provide for thame; whiche, without wisdome, ar more abill to be thair ruyne [5] and confusioun, than help or comfort. And as this is most treu, so we leave it with the rest of the commoditeis to be weyit by your Honouris wisdome, and set fordwart by your authoritie

[1] Burden and withdraw.
[2] Without trouble.
[3] Affairs.
[4] Than any.
[5] Ruin.

to the most heigh advancement of this Common-wealth, committed to your charge.

KNOX'S VIEW OF GOVERNMENT [1]

Of the Civile Magistrat

We Confesse and acknawledge impyres, kyngdomes, dominiounis, and cities to be distincted and ordaned by God: the powers and authorities in the same (be it of Emperouris in thair impyris, of Kingis in thair realmes, Dukis and Princes in thair dominiounis, or of otheris Magistratis in free cities,) to be Godis holy ordinance, ordeaned for manifestatioun of his awin glorie, and for the singulare proffeit and commodite of mankynd. So that whosoever goes about to tack away or to confound the haill state of civile policies, now lang establisched, we affirme the same men not onlie to be ennemyes to mankynd, but also wickedlie to feght against Godis expressed will. We farther Confesse and acknawledge, that sic personis as are placed in authoritie are to be loved, honoured, feared, and holdin in most reverent estimatioun; becaus (that) thei are the lieutennentis of God, in whose sessioun God him self doeth sitt and judge, (yea evin the Judges and Princes thame selfis,) to whome by God is gevin the sweard, to the praise and defence of good men, and to revenge and puniss all open malefactouris. Moreover, to Kingis, Princes, Reullaris, and Magistratis, we affirme that cheiflie and maist principallie the reforma-

[1] LAING, DAVID, "The Works of John Knox," Vol. II, pp. 118–119.

tioun [1] and purgatioun of the Religioun apperteanes; so that
not onlie thei are appointed for civile policey, bot also for
mantenance of the trew Religioun, and for suppressing of
idolatrie and superstitioun whatsomever, as in David, Josa-
phat, Ezechias, Josias, and otheris, heychtlie commended for
thair zeall in that caise, may be espyed. And thairfoir we confesse and avow, that sick as resist the Supreme power, (doing
that thing which apperteanis to his charge,) do resist Goddis
ordinance, and thairfoir can not be guyltless. And farther,
we affirme, that whosoever deny unto thame thair aid,
counsall, and conforte, while the Princes and Reullaris vigi-
lantlie travaill in the executing [2] of thair office, that the same
men deny thair help, supporte, and counsall to God, who by
the presence of his lieutennent craveth it of thame.

TEACHING OF THE CATECHISM ON SUNDAY [3]

But the Sunday must straitlie be keipit, both before and
efter noon, in all tounis. Before noon, must the word be
preached and sacramentis ministered, as also Mariage
solempnissed, yf occasion offer: After noon must the young
children be publictlie examined in thair Catechisme in au-
dience of the pepill, in doing whairof the Minister must tak
gret deligence, alsweill [4] to cause the Pepill to understand

[1] In the old printed copies, "conservatioun."
[2] In the old printed copies, "in executioun."
[3] LAING, DAVID, "The Works of John Knox," Vol. II, pp. 238–
239.
[4] As well.

the questionis proponed, as the ansueiris,[1] and the doctrine
that may be collected thairof. The ordour and how much
is appointed for everie Sunday, is alreaddy distinctit in oure
buke of Common Ordour; whiche Catechism is the most
perfite that ever yit was used in the Churche. At efter noon
also may Baptisme be ministered, whan occasioun is offered
of great travell before noon. It is also to be observit, that
prayeris be used at after noon upoun the Sunday, whair
thair is neathir preching nor catechisme.

BIBLE READING, FAMILY INSTRUCTION, SINGING [2]

Farthir, we think it a thing most expedient and necessarie,
that everie Churche have a Bibill in Inglische, and that the
people be commanded to convene to heir the plane reiding
or interpretatioun of the Scripturis, as the Churche shall appoint; that be frequent reiding this gross ignorance, whiche
in the cursit Papistrie hath overflowne all, may partlie be re-
movit. We think it most expedient that the Scripturis be red
in ordour, that is, that some one buke of the Auld and the
New Testament be begun and ordourlie red to the end. And
the same we judge of preching, whair the Minister for [the]
maist part remaneth in one place: For this skipping and
divagatioun frome place to place of the Scripture, be it in
reiding, or be it in precheing, we judge not so proffitabill

[1] Answers.
[2] LAING, DAVID, "The Works of John Knox," Vol. II, pp. 240–
241.

to edifie the Churche, as the continewall following of ane text.

Everie Maister of houshald must be commandit eathir to instruct, or ellis caus [to] be instructed, his children, servandis, and familie, in the principallis of the Christiane religioun; without the knawledge whairof aught none to be admitted to the Tabill of the Lord Jesus: for suche as be so dull and so ignorant, that thei can neathir try thame selfis, neathir yit know the dignitie and misterie of that actioun, can not eat and drink of that Tabill worthelie. And thairfore of necessistie we judge it, that everie yeare at least, publict examinatioun be had by the Ministeris and Elderis of the knawledge of everie persoun within the Churche; to wit, that everie maister and maistres of houshald cum thame selvis and thair familie so many as be cum to maturitie, before the Ministeris and Elderis, to gyf confessioun of thair faith, and to ansueir to such cheaf points of Religioun as the Ministeris shall demand. Such as be ignorant in the Articulis of thair Faith; understand not, nor can not rehearse the Commandimentis of God; knaw not how to pray; neathir whairinto thair richtousnes consistis, aught not to be admitted to the Lordis Tabill. And gif thay stuburnlie continew, and suffer thair children and servandis to continew in wilfull ignorance, the discipline of the Churche must proceid against them unto excommunicatioun; and than must the mater be referred to the Civill Magistrat. For seing that the just levith be his awin faith, and that Christ Jesus justifieth be knawledge off him self, insufferable we judge it that men shall be permitted to leve and continew

tinew in ignorance as memberis of the Churche of God.

Moreover, men, wemen, and children wald be exhorted to exercise thame selvis in the Psalmes, that when the Churche convenith, and dois sing, thai may be the more abill togither with commoun heart and voice to prayse God.

In private housses we think it expedient, that the most grave and discrete persoun use the Commoun Prayeris at morne and at nycht, for the confort and instructioun of uthiris. For seing that we behald and se the hand of God now presentlie striking us with diverse plagues, we think it ane contempt of his judgementis, or any provocatioun of his anger more to be kendillit against us, yf we be not movit to repentence of oure formar unthankfulnes, and to earnist invocatioun of His name, whois onlie power may, (and great mercy will,) yff we unfeynedlie convert unto him, remove from us these terribill plagues whiche now for our in-iquiteis hing oure our headis. "Convert us, O Lord, and we shall be converted."

A Prayer to be said of the Childe, before He
Studie his Lesson [1]

Out of the 119 Psalme.—Wherein shal the Child addresse his way? in guiding himselfe according to thy worde. Open myne eyes, and I shal knowe the merveiles of thy Law. Give me understanding, and I shal kepe thy Law, yea I shal kepe it with mine whole heart.

[1] Laing, David, "The Works of John Knox," Vol. VI, pp. 358–359 (translation of Calvin's catechism).

Lord, which art the fountaine of all wisedome and knowledge, seeing it hath pleased thee to give me the meane to
be taught in my youth, for to learne to guide me godly and
honestly all the course of my life; it may also please thee
to lighten myne understanding (the which of it selfe is
blinde), that it may comprehend and receive that doctrine
and learning which shalbe taught me: it may please thee
to strengthen my memorie to kepe it well; it may please
thee also to dispose myne hearte willinglie to receive it with
suche desire as apperteineth, so that by myne ingratitude,
the occasion which thou givest me, be not lost. That I may
thus do, it may please thee to powre upon me thyne Holie
Sprit, the Sprit, I say, of all understanding, trueth, judge-
ment, wisdome, and learning, the which may make me able
so to profite, that the paines that shalbe taken in teaching
me be not in vaine. And to what studie so ever I apply my
selfe, make me, O Lord, to addresse it unto the right end:
that is, to knowe thee in our Lord Jesus Christ, that I may
have ful trust of salvation in thy grace, and to serve thee
uprightly according to thy pleasure, so that whatsoever I
learne, it may be unto me as an instrument to help me there-
unto.

And seing thou dost promise to give wisdome to the lytle
and humble ones, and to confounde the proude in the vanitie
of their wits, and lykewise to make thy selfe knowen to them
that be of an upright heart, and also to blynde the ungodly
and wicked; I beseech thee to facion me unto true humilitie,
so that I may be taught first to be obedient unto thee, and
next unto my superiors, that thou hast appointed over me:

further, that it may please thee to dispose mine heart un-
feinedly to seke thee, and to forsake all evil and filthie
lustes of the flesh: And that in this sorte, I may now prepare my selfe to serve thee once in that estate which it shal
please thee to appoint for me, when I shal come to age.

Out of the 25 Psalme.—The Lord reveileth his secrets
unto them that feare him, and maketh them to knowe his
alliance.

JOHN LOCKE

THE ANABAPTISTS

ANABAPTIST EDUCATIONAL INFLUENCES

THE Anabaptists were the Ishmaelites of modern Europe. The name was held in bitter reproach, and many and prolonged were the efforts to effect their extermination. They continued, however, to exist in diverse and scattered bodies below the surface of the social and political strata of central European lands. Under the more liberal governments of the Netherlands and England they began to emerge, and finally, in America, their doctrinal descendants gave to civilization their most important contributions. Apart from their more theological tenets, they contended consistently for individual religious liberty and for the absolute separation of church and state. Their emphatic recognition of the individual conscience and of the equality of all men before God has done much to make American democracy. Their insistence upon the New Testament and church membership based upon individual responsibility naturally stressed the reading of the Scriptures. For higher education they cared less; in fact they felt that learned men had misled the people and misinterpreted the divine revelation and could not be trusted. More than that, pride of learning and intellect was just as evil as any other form of pride and was repellant to true Christian humility. Having no state government to establish and support schools, they did not soon establish any institutions for instruction.

The excerpt presented here gives their doctrine of the state, or the "sword," as they thought of it. The great majority of these people were absolute pacifists and not only declined to fight for the state but practiced non-resistance.

LETTER OF THE BROTHERLY UNION OF CERTAIN BELIEVING BAPTIZED CHILDREN OF GOD, WHO HAVE ASSEMBLED AT SCHLEITHEIM, TO THE CONGREGATIONS OF BELIEVING, BAPTIZED CHRISTIANS:

Translated by Thomas Armitage [1]

. . . .

6. Sixthly, we were united concerning the sword, thus: The sword is an ordinance of God outside of the perfection of Christ, which punishes and slays the wicked and protects and guards the good. In law the sword is ordained over the wicked for punishment and death, and the civil power is ordained to use it. But in the perfection of Christ, excommunication is pronounced only for warning and for exclusion of him who has sinned, without death of the flesh, only by warning and the command not to sin again. It is asked by many who do not know the will of Christ respecting us, whether a Christian may or should use the sword against the wicked in order to protect and guard the good, or for love?

The answer is unanimously revealed thus: Christ teaches and commands us that we should learn from him, for he is

[1] ARMITAGE, THOMAS, "History of the Baptists," pp. 949–952.

meek and lowly of heart, and so we will find rest for our souls. Now, Christ says to the heathen woman who was taken in adultery, not that they should stone her according to the law of his Father (yet he also said, "as the Father gave me commandment, even so I do"), but in mercy, and forgiveness, and warning to sin no more, and says, "Go and sin no more." So should we also closely follow according to the law of excommunication.

Secondly, It is asked concerning the sword, whether a Christian should pronounce judgment in worldly disputes and quarrels which unbelievers have with one another? The only answer is: Christ was not willing to decide or judge between brothers concerning inheritance, but refused to do it; so should we also do.

Thirdly, It is asked concerning the sword, Should one be a magistrate if he is elected thereto? To this the answer is: It was intended to make Christ a King, and he fled and did not disregard the ordinance of his Father. Thus should we do and follow him, and we shall not walk in darkness. For he himself says, "Whosoever will come after me, let him deny himself and take up his cross and follow me." Also, he himself forbids the power of the sword and says, "The princes of the Gentiles exercise lordship," etc., "but it shall not be so among you." Further, Paul says, "for whom he did foreknow he also did predestinate to be conformed to the image of his son." Also, Peter says, "Christ has suffered (not ruled), leaving us an ensample that ye should follow his steps."

Lastly, it is remarked that it does not become a Christian to be a magistrate for these reasons: The rule of the magistrate is according to the flesh, that of the Christian according to the Spirit; their houses and dwelling remain in this world, the Christian's is in heaven; their citizenship is in this world, the Christian's citizenship is in heaven; the weapons of their contest and war are carnal and only against the flesh, but the weapons of the Christian are spiritual, against the fortresses of the devil; the worldly are armed with steel and iron, but the Christians are armed with the armor of God, with truth, righteousness, peace, faith, salvation, and with the word of God. In short, as Christ our head was minded towards us, so should the members of the body of Christ through him be minded, that there be no schism in the body by which it be destroyed. For every kingdom divided against itself will be brought to destruction. Therefore, as Christ is, as it stands written of him, so must the members be, that his body be whole and one, to the edification of itself.

7. Seventhly, we were united concerning oaths, thus: The oath is an assurance among those who dispute or promise, and was spoken of in the law that it should take place with the name of God, only in truth and not in falsehood. Christ, who teaches the perfection of the law, forbids to his people all swearing, whether true or false, neither by heaven nor by earth, nor by Jerusalem, nor by our head, and that for the reason which he immediately after gives, "Because thou canst not make one hair white or black." Take heed, all swearing is therefore forbidden, because we are not able to make good that which is promised in the oath, since we

cannot change the least thing upon us. Now, there are some who do not believe the simple command of God, but they speak and ask thus: If God swore to Abraham by himself because he was God (when he promised him that he would do good to him and would be his God if he kept his commands), why should I not also swear if I promise a person something? Answer. Hear what the Scripture says: "God being willing more abundantly to shew unto the heirs of promise the immutability of his counsel, confirmed it with an oath, that by two immutable things, in which it was impossible for God to lie, we might have a strong consolation." Mark the meaning of this Scripture: God has power to do what he forbids to you, for to him all things are possible.

"God swore an oath to Abraham," says the Scripture, "in order that he might show his counsel to be immutable"; that is, no one can withstand or hinder his will, and therefore he can keep the oath. But, as was said by Christ above, "We have no power either to hold or to give," and therefore should not swear at all.

Further, some say God has not forbidden in the New Testament to swear, and he has commanded it in the Old; but it is only forbidden to swear by heaven, earth, Jerusalem, and by our head. Answer. Hear the Scriptures: "He that shall swear by heaven sweareth by the throne of God; and by him that sitteth thereon." Mark, swearing by heaven is forbidden, which is only the throne of God; how much more is it forbidden to swear by God himself! Ye fools and blind, which is the greater, the throne, or he who sits upon it?

Still, some say, If it is wrong to use God's name for the truth, yet the apostles, Peter and Paul, swore. Answer. Peter and Paul testify only that which God promised to Abraham by oath, and they themselves promised nothing, as the examples clearly show. But to testify and to swear are different things. When one swears he promises a thing in the future, as Christ was promised to Abraham, whom we received a long time afterwards. When one testifies he witnesses concerning that which is present, whether it be good or bad, as Simon spoke of Christ to Mary and testified, "Behold, this one is set for the fall and rising of many in Israel, and for a sign which shall be spoken against." Similarly Christ has taught us when he says, "Let your communication be yea, yea, nay, nay; for whatsoever is more than these cometh of the Evil One." He says, your speech or word shall be yea and nay, and his intention is clear.

Christ is simple yea and nay, and all who seek him simply will understand his word. Amen.

. . ..

The name of God be eternally praised and glorified. Amen.

The Lord give you his peace. Amen.

ACTA SCHLAITTEN AM RANDEN AUF MATTHIAE,[1] *February 24th, Anno* MCXXVII.

[1] Proceedings in Schlaitten on the Randen on Saint Matthias' Day.

INDEX

INDEX

Classes, 199 ff., 213, 259 ff.
  (*See also* Groups.)
Clerical office, 109-110
Cloister schools, 72, 76, 98, 214, 219 ff.
  (*See also* Cloister.)
Collegiate churches, 75
Commandments, 88, 89, 93 ff., 96
Common People, 45, 87, 88, 121
Commonwealth, 280, 288, 291
Compulsory education, 85, 149-150
Concordia Publishing House, 45
"Confession of Faith," 266, 267
Copernican system, 3, 163
Cordier, 233
Curricula, 162, 259 ff., 280-281

D

Daily program, 256-258
Demosthenes, 169
Depravity, 236 ff.
Devil, 48 ff., 50, 58, 71, 84, 95, 101-102, 113, 114, 115
Dialectic, 12, 162, 200, 253, 281, 282
Discipline, 12, 22 ff., 28, 31, 33, 69, 84, 100
Disputation, 37
Donatus, 71, 182
Dutch Reformed, 235
Dwellings, 198-199

E

Economics, 282
Elders, 250

Elementary education, 98-99, 234-235
Elementary German schools, 204 ff., 214
Elementary instruction, 182, 194 ff.
Emmanuel College, 253
Endowments, 83, 85, 98, 121, 288
Erasmus, 11, 13, 14, 43, 183
Ethics, 36, 163, 282, 284
Examination, 222-223, 235

F

Family government, 79 ff., 293
  (*See also* Discipline.)
Faulkner, 14
Flogging, 12, 31, 70
Frederick, Duke of Saxony, 81, 130, 167
French, 259

G

Geneva, 234, 235, 273, 275
Geometric, 282
George of Brandenberg, 98
German, 20, 51, 60, 153, 162, 165, 166-167, 180, 181
German books, 122
German language, 15
German schools, 180, 211, 224, 228-229
Germans, 57, 78
Germany, 58, 148, 149, 192
Girls, 68, 71, 180, 192, 224, 228, 229-230
Girls' schools, 41, 204 ff., 212
Glasgow University, 281, 285

308

INDEX

309

INDEX

INDEX

INDEX

370408
E169
39131